NOT THIS WIDOW

A Journey of Grief:
Love, Loss, Strength and Survival

by Dilys Sillah

Conscious Dreams
PUBLISHING

Not This Widow

Copyright ©2024: Dilys Sillah

All rights reserved. No part of this publication may be produced, distributed, or transmitted in photocopying, recording, or other electronic or mechanical methods, any form or by any means, including without the prior written permission of the publisher, except in the case of brief quotations embodied in critical reviews and certain other non-commercial uses permitted by copyright law.

This is a work of fiction. Names, characters, businesses, places, events and incidents are either the products of the author's imagination or used in a fictitious manner. Any resemblance to actual persons, living or dead, or actual events is purely coincidental.

First Printed in United Kingdom, 2020

Published by Conscious Dreams Publishing
www.consciousdreamspublishing.com

Edited by Rhoda Molife
www.molahmedia.com

Typeset by Oksana Kosovan

ISBN: 978-1-915522-65-8

Dedication

To my darling husband Edward Sillah – none of this would have been possible without you. You gave me a life worth writing about and paid the ultimate price for me to have a story to tell. You would have been so proud of me. I know how chuffed you were when I wrote *Predator or Prince*. You set up a WhatsApp group just to tell your friends! This time you're not here but I am, and I hope I have made you proud again.

With all my love, from the very depths of my soul, thank you Eddie.

Thank you.

Contents

Chapter 1
The One 7

Chapter 2
Happily Ever After... 19

Chapter 3
Shattered Dreams.. 31

Chapter 4
The Battle.. 41

Chapter 5
Return to Base 53

Chapter 6
Home Sweet Home 61

Chapter 7
Darkness.. 75

Chapter 8
The Loud Silent War 87

Chapter 9
Over the Rainbow 99

Chapter 10
A Kiss Goodnight.. 111

Chapter 11
Gone But Not Forgotten 117

Chapter 12
The Incoherence of Grief.. 127

Chapter 13
Death Respects No Person.. 141

Chapter 14
Afi's Story.. 143

Chapter 15
Rachel's Story 151

Chapter 16
Anne's Story 165

Chapter 17
Penelope's Story.. 177

Chapter 18
To Whom It May Concern... 185

Chapter 19
A Penny for Your Thoughts 203

Chapter 20
New Beginnings 211

Chapter 1

The One

One of my sisters had always said to me, "Dilys, as soon as you leave your job, you're going to meet your husband."

I have no idea why my sister thought this but somehow it turned out that she was right.

I had been working in a local authority in north-west London for about six years when I decided I needed a change. I was so unhappy toward the end of that era, I knew I couldn't continue as I was. It wasn't unusual to wake up with feelings of dread and anxiety at the thought of having to walk into a busy and hostile environment with little or no support to get through the working day.

There were so many things I'd wanted to do at that time and one of them was to pursue my singing career. I was singing around the West End and doing backing vocal sessions here and there, but the truth is, that was what I really wanted to do and I needed to allow myself the chance to explore my dreams. I figured if I gave up my full-time permanent role to contract instead, it would give me the flexibility to be able to take leave when I wanted so I could sing and do gigs without the nine-to-five restrictions. So, I began the quest of looking for contract work that would give me what I needed.

Even though I had planned to leave my job, there was still that feeling of uncertainty and fear of the unknown and I questioned if I was really doing the right thing. Although I was offered five contracting roles, I still didn't make the leap to hand in my notice and take up those offers. I knew I couldn't keep turning jobs down when one of the agencies called to offer a contract that required me to start in two weeks. This was the same agency that was responsible for offering me two of the jobs that I had turned down already.

I thought, *If I turn down this one as well, I can kiss this contracting dream goodbye.* I'm sure it wasn't my imagination hearing the slight irritation in the consultant's voice from the agency. I knew if I didn't take it they would think I wasn't serious and probably not place me in any other roles, so I took the plunge, handed in my notice and began working at Wandsworth Council in July 2002.

My role working in the Housing Benefit and Council Tax Department began; little did I know that there was a gentleman working there by the name of Edward Sillah who would become my husband.

★★★

I remember this very tall, dark and handsome man coming over to me to introduce himself and asking my name. Having told him my name was Dilys, he replied by saying, "Dele?" I looked at him, scoffed and said, "No! Dilys!" He extended his hand for me to shake, which I did and that was that.

Chapter 1. The One

Over the subsequent weeks we would chat and exchange pleasantries. I was not looking for a relationship, so I was absolutely, not even remotely interested in pursuing any kind of office romance at that time. However, Eddie, as he was popularly known, had other ideas.

It wasn't too long before he discovered my weak spot – good food! I absolutely loved and still do love great cuisine and Eddie could cook! He would come into work with various dishes, all delicious, that I would enjoy for lunch. He would pack two lunch boxes, one for me and one for himself, and plonk mine on my desk while I was deep in conversation with a customer, telling them why they had lost their right to pay their council tax in instalments. The once-attentive customer services rep was now distracted by king prawns and spicy couscous!

These little gestures opened up the opportunity for us to talk more and get to know each other. He would often give me a ride if I needed to get anywhere and was generally always there if I needed anything.

One thing I used to find sweet and amusing would be that every time I sat in his car, he would just happen to be playing a song that would somehow describe his feelings towards me or our friendship. I know some people might think this was cheesy but the way he did it was actually quite slick. I remember one occasion after we had been talking for quite some time, he just happened to be playing a song by Mario, 'Just a Friend'. This song was about a guy who had met a girl and wanted to know everything about her with the view of having a deep and meaningful relationship with her; the only thing was that the object of his desires seemed to only see him as friend and nothing else. It was so apt in describing the situation he felt he was in that I just laughed in my head as I took my seat in his BMW. By now about three months had passed but I realised I was actually falling for this guy too.

***

After one of our normal days at work, Eddie had given me a lift home and I invited him in. I was living in Finchley which was quite a long drive from work. I knew he was a gentleman so there was nothing to worry about if he was in my space. We chatted for a while after having something to eat; it was then that he told me he loved me.

At the time I was going to church and had beliefs I felt were important to me. These needed to be considered if I was going to enter into a relationship with anybody. One of them was that the person would also have to be a Christian and be prepared to come to church as it was a huge part of my life. I was one of the praise and worship leaders in my church and I knew it would be virtually impossible to be with somebody who was against being in that kind of environment or holding the same or similar beliefs. So, my little test for all guys was to invite them to church and see their reaction. I knew if that suggestion had a guy's head doing a 360, or I could smell burning, he probably wasn't the one for me.

So, I told Mr Eddie that if he really was interested in me, he would have to come to church. To my surprise, he didn't hesitate; he accepted and followed me to the mid-week service on a Thursday evening when I was leading praise and worship. Until that point, Eddie wasn't aware I could sing, and

Chapter 1. The One

I remember singing and seeing his face looking both shocked, proud and pleasantly surprised.

It was around this time that he shared with me that he was brought up by his grandfather in Sierra Leone, where he was born. His grandfather, Reverend Warritay was the first reverend minister of Sierra Leone. Eddie spoke very highly and fondly of him and the upbringing he received, telling me it had moulded him into the man he was. Based on my own background, this was quite encouraging, and I felt it was something that would give us a solid foundation to build on. I wasn't done though; I had a further test for Eddie because by this time, I felt I actually did want to settle down and was ready for marriage; after all, I was 31.

I had a conversation with Eddie and told him I wanted to settle down, get married and was not looking for a boyfriend; if it was a boyfriend I was looking for, he certainly wouldn't have found me single. It's not like I was short of offers but I knew what I wanted at that time and I really wanted to have a family of my own. I've never been a believer in the woman having to wait to be chosen; I strongly believe a woman should do the choosing. By that, I don't mean she necessarily has to go out and pursue men but that a woman should be able to confidently put out there what it is she is looking for without feeling she should either have to play it cool for fear of frightening the man off or fear of looking desperate. I was neither desperate nor eager to be married for the wrong reasons but I certainly knew I was ready for marriage. It was only right I laid my cards on the table for any man that showed an interest in me.

My philosophy had always been that if the man runs scared, he isn't ready and isn't the man for you, in which case you save yourself a lot of time, trouble and heartache. I've always felt sad for women who stay in relationships without having stated what it is they wanted, then go on to live on a hope and prayer that one day the man they are with will pop the question. I was never wired that way and absolutely refused to give the most precious commodity any human being, especially women, possessed – time – to a man who may not necessarily share the same dreams and aspirations.

I remember Eddie pausing and saying, yes, of course he would like to settle down and get married too. I don't know if he genuinely did want to get married or whether it was the shock of my very direct, no-nonsense approach. Maybe it was the fact that he knew I was a serious person and if he said anything other than what I had wanted, I may not have continued a relationship with him. However, it seemed that on the very day he saw me when I walked through the doors of Wandsworth Council in July 2002, one of his work colleagues had pointed me out to him and asked if he had seen the new girl who had started in the office. Eddie said he had and boldly declared to them, "I'm going to marry that girl!" They all laughed apparently and said, "Yeah, right!"

***

Well, we ended up getting married three years later, in July 2005. I remember having six months to plan the wedding because we spontaneously decided we were going to get married before the year was out. I found a lovely venue in Hertfordshire which had beautiful grounds and I thought

Chapter 1. The One

to myself this was definitely where I would want to have my wedding. I've always been quite good at planning events so I relied very much on my expertise to get things done, because I thought it would be easier and less stressful to do as much as I could for myself.

We found the church, set the date and were good to go. I remember being really happy with the church we found and arranged to meet the vicar. He was a bit brash, but I thought little of it. We had a few meetings to discuss the organist, the running order of the ceremony and the finer details of the wedding. One evening, as we discussed the wedding, I told Eddie that I had a funny feeling about the vicar. I felt he was a bit short with some of the elderly parishioners when he spoke to them and had witnessed a few curt answers to some of them during our tea and cake time; it played on my mind a bit.

Now I've always said I'm never wrong about people, and I'm still yet to eat my words when summing up anyone that comes into my space. It's both a curse and a blessing to always be right about humans. When everyone else feels someone is super-wonderful, I'll be the one saying, "I'm not sure" when really, I'm damn certain and just trying to give others time to catch up!

I've always been a big believer in trusting your intuition and listening to your sixth sense. Intuition is there for a reason, but most people just think they're being silly and explain that niggling feeling away. Then when what they felt unsettled about manifests, they wished they could have turned back the hands of time and trusted themselves to begin with. Since childhood I'd always adopted an attitude of self-belief and trusted my instincts; I learn quickly and a few experiences taught me very quickly to pay attention when my antenna goes up about a person or a situation.

So everything was running relatively smoothly in terms of planning, up to the time of the wedding. There was one thing though that was crucial and still had to be sorted out, and that was the order of service.

Now, as stereotypical as this may sound, and this will probably be the most controversial thing I'm going to say: Africans are generally not known for their punctuality when it comes to attending functions. There's a necessary evil we live with, an unspoken rule almost, that when a party, wedding or function has been arranged, you can arrive late because everybody else is going to be late! So, people generally don't want to be the first one sitting there waiting for everybody else to arrive. For this reason, I made the decision to change the start time on the order of service from 1 o'clock to 12:15 to ensure the guests' punctuality. I then sent the order of service to the vicar to confirm.

★★★

I was on the train coming back from Ealing when I received a call from him. He was raving mad. It actually took me a few moments to realise that it was him on the line, and that he knew he was speaking to me and hadn't misdialled. What I recall him screaming like a banshee down the phone was, "How dare you change the time on the order of service! How dare you change the time of the order of service for my church!"

Chapter 1. The One

To say I was gobsmacked is an understatement. Calmly, I tried to get a word in edgeways to explain my reasons for changing the time.

"I don't care if it's an African wedding. I don't care. You have no right to change the time on the order of service. How dare you? I have a good mind to cancel the wedding!" he continued shouting.

The little I'd seen of the vicar's character and attitude left me with no doubt he would have indeed cancelled the wedding. The way he was screaming led me to believe he wanted me to say something that would justify him in doing that, even though the wedding was only two weeks away. The only thing I said in response to his screams and disrespect was that I would not permit him to continue to speak to me that way. God knows why I was on the train that was soon to enter the underground, because I would have really told him what I thought. As the good Lord would have it, there was a female vicar who had just been ordained. At a prior meeting about the wedding, it was agreed she would officiate the wedding and not him. I was so relieved when I recalled this because I couldn't imagine having somebody that had such little regard for others officiating at my wedding.

★★★

D-Day finally arrived, and I was alarmingly calm. I spent the night before at a small and cosy hotel near one of my sister's homes. In the morning, my make-up artist arrived and by the time I was in my dress with my hair and make-up done, I'd been transformed into a bride. I was walking on air.

It rained, which I was told at the time was a sign of a blessed marriage. Most brides pray for blue skies and sunshine but on the previous day, it had been so hot that I was worried how I would cope with a full gown, tights and tiara; I was grateful for the rain and all that it symbolised.

I walked down the aisle to 'Ave Maria', to meet a nervous groom. The officiating vicar made a shambles of telling the story of how we met, stating I was 'unemployed' at the time! Oh, the embarrassment! It made it look like the version we had told our families and friends was a total fabrication but we did laugh about it later. What it meant was that our wedding video had to be heavily edited to remove all parts that told that crucial story; something I do feel is a shame now.

★★★

We went on to have a series of celebrations on the days following until we boarded our flight for a ten-night luxury honeymoon in Mauritius. It was one of the best times we spent together on holiday. During our stay, I celebrated my birthday too. I had no idea how Eddie managed to arrange a surprise private champagne dinner for two on the beach, have rose petals scattered over the floor and on the bed in our hotel suite, along with champagne on ice for our return.

The funny thing was, Eddie didn't drink. He had never had a smoke or a drink in his life, yet he would indulge me in my love for champagne and a good cocktail. He would often tease me by calling me a 'wine bibber' whenever I drank. We had an agreement that if alcohol was being served, he wouldn't say he didn't drink; instead, he'd accept the offer and order what

Chapter 1. The One

I liked, hold the drink as authentically as possible and then pass it to me once I was done with mine. I would pass my empty glass to him as if he'd finished his drink and then polish his off. It worked like a dream on the plane when we were congratulated by the air hostesses with glasses of champagne!

We had an amazing time and always said we would return, but never managed to. I do have a piece of Mauritius with me though and great memories of my birthday and the beautiful diamond eternity ring Eddie had given me as a present.

★★★

Married life really started when we touched down eleven days later at Gatwick. For some odd reason, we hadn't booked a minicab to take us home; instead, we took the Gatwick Express and lugged two heavy suitcases on the London Underground. I felt a bit unwell and couldn't understand for the life of me why we were doing this. I knew if I was travelling solo, that would never have happened. Oh no. I book my transportation when I book my flights whenever I'm going away but I guess I realised this is what it's like when there's the habits of someone else to consider and not just your own. This was the new world of compromise, compromise, comprise that we're told of when we get married.

Chapter 2

Happily Ever After

Whenever you bring two completely different characters together under one roof, you have got to expect that some work will have to be done. Eddie and I had a good marriage but, of course, not without its challenges.

On the surface, I was the outgoing life and soul of the party and Eddie was, supposedly, the more reserved of the two of us. The truth is Eddie had a huge personality, an excellent and sharp wit (he was great at telling jokes) and would hold court often when we were out. He was highly intelligent and could speak on any topic to do with current affairs and history; I learnt a lot from him. Eddie was a terrible wind-up merchant and could tease you till the cows came home. He loved to talk, and we spent a lot of time doing that. The one thing we both had in common was a love of staying indoors! Yes, who would believe that?

I'm often seen as a social butterfly, but I honestly love my own company, to the point of being considered a bit too much. I love solitude and silence and even as I write, my house is in complete silence but for the helicopter flying overhead and the sound of my need-to-get-my-manicure-done nails tapping away on my laptop. If Eddie were here, as I'm sitting on his part of our leather sofa, the TV would be on and he would be on his phone and guarding both remote controls to the TV and satellite box. He was the man of the house and of course, every woman knows it's a man's God-given right to hog the remote control, even if they are fast asleep and not even watching the damn thing! Eddie liked a bit of noise, whereas I was so noise averse.

I remember when we first got married, we had a major battle in the bedroom and no, it's not what you might be thinking! Eddie's love for TV meant he was used to sleeping with it on. I on the other hand hate any form of light when I'm trying to sleep – it reminds me of prisoners of war being tortured with light bulbs going on and off when they're trying to catch some shut-eye in between being electrocuted. Dramatic I know, but this is exactly how I felt; I nearly expected to be waterboarded during the night – that's how bad it was.

Something you would think was so minor was a huge deal so I often had to wait for Eddie to fall asleep, then I could switch off the TV. The number of times I wanted to fling the telly out of the window plus that blasted Sky box with the little green flashing light, you will never know. Eventually we were able to compromise, and the agreement was the TV went off at midnight, otherwise he could watch it in the living room and then come to bed and do what you're supposed to do in the bedroom, aside from the obvious, and that was to sleep!

What really helped was pre-marital counselling, which I think was good for us.

Chapter 2. Happily Ever After

Our pastor at the time would meet with us every week up until the wedding to counsel us. We would go through different areas known to be contentious within marriage if not dealt with and he would present different scenarios for us to discuss. He would work out how we communicated with each other, based on our responses.

We covered finances, how to resolve conflict, what type of marriage we wanted, whether traditional or modern, that sort of thing. Some people thought it strange to have pre-marital counselling but looking at the rate of divorce and dysfunctional homes, I'm surprised it's not encouraged more. I came to understand a few things about my husband that were helpful. For example, I hate things to fester and don't like there to be an atmosphere because of a disagreement. For me, it's important to talk things over, get it out of the way and move on. Eddie on the other hand needed time to deal with whatever had upset him on his own before he would be open to discuss. This was a huge eye-opener for me and the suggestion by our pastor on how to compromise on that was excellent. He told me to allow Eddie space to process whatever it was that was going on but, and there was a big but, we were not only barred from going to bed angry but also had to talk about the issue, discuss a solution and agree a way forward. I can't say we always practised what we learnt, but at least we were taught and were given the necessary tools to deal with that aspect of our marriage.

★★★

Very early into our marriage, we were faced with the trauma of my miscarriage. I had always known I would conceive on our wedding night; it's just one of those feelings I'd always had. When we returned from our honeymoon, one of my cousins was getting married. I was wearing a lovely sky-blue dress I had made for my 30th birthday and thought it would be nice to wear it to such a special occasion.

I couldn't understand why I was bleeding and because of the wedding planning and honeymoon, I wasn't paying attention to my dates. It was only after a couple of days that I saw my doctor and she confirmed I had miscarried at seven or eight weeks. To say I devastated is an understatement. It was such a shock and yet I kept telling myself I should have known. Eddie remained quiet when I broke the news to him. He hugged me and eventually said not to worry and that we would try again.

I already had a son who was 12 when Eddie and I got married. Having had a traumatic labour with him, nearly losing my life in the process, I really didn't want any more children until I had met and married Eddie. Church had a lot to do with that decision too in that my mindset had changed and I realised having a horrible experience didn't mean it had to repeat itself.

A few months later, I fell pregnant with our daughter. I knew the day I conceived that I was pregnant – I just knew it. I took a pregnancy test four days before I was due to because I was so sure and, lo and behold, I saw those two pink lines confirming what I already knew. I also instinctively knew I was going to have a girl.

Wondering how I would break the happy news to Eddie, I decided to buy a little white cardigan with pink ribbons on it and a pair of pink booties. I placed the items in a gift bag, plus the pregnancy test results, and handed them to him when he got back from work. The look on his face was priceless and he gave me a huge hug with no tears this time. We were consumed with utter joy and elation that we were going to be parents again and we knew everything was going to be all right.

I bought a book called *Supernatural Childbirth* by Jackie Mize that became my pregnancy bible. I carried that book with me *everywhere* and read it over and over. This amazing book was about the author herself, who was told she couldn't have children, but ended up having four beautiful ones, defying all that the doctors had told her. She was a Christian woman, and she meditated on certain parts of The Bible to push her faith to the limit and prove everyone wrong. This wonderful book covered words of affirmation from The Bible, spoke about miscarriage and even about how women can have relatively pain-free births with an easy and quick labour – two major elements that eluded me when I had my son.

***

When I was giving birth to my son, labour lasted for three days. I nearly died as a result of blood loss and he was stuck in my pelvis. I also received the most horrendous care from the hospital. One memory I have is of asking the ward sister for pain relief. She was a horrible woman who never smiled or reassured anyone but just pranced around the ward with a stern look on her face. She came onto the ward to do her rounds and checked my stitches quickly before barking at me, saying they were fine and confirming that I could be discharged. I could hardly move yet she refused to give me any pain relief. Worried because I needed to get my baby a bottle of milk that was quite a distance from the ward, I attempted to get up, albeit a little shakily. I managed to make it to the front desk; surprisingly there was nobody there. At this point, I took a few more steps and collapsed onto the floor – a pathetic, crying, crumpled heap. It was one of the new dads who found me and called for help. I was placed in a wheelchair and taken back to bed.

The old witch came to the ward, poked her head round the door and shouted. "Next time make her walk!"

I was too weak and too distraught to respond. The following day, the same sister went around the ward discharging the mothers she felt were fit to go home. When she got to me, I told her she was in the wrong job and should be an undertaker and that she had no business working with people who were still breathing. The look on her face was a picture; forget *Fifty Shades of Grey*, this was Fifty Shades of Red! The other mothers loved me for that little outburst, and I was glad I was able to release a little of the frustration I felt.

So, my experience some 14 years prior, plus a miscarriage, didn't bring back particularly fond memories of pregnancy and childbirth for me. Around 12 weeks into the pregnancy with my daughter, I began to bleed. This time it was different because I knew I was pregnant, and I just prayed I would be okay.

I told Eddie what was happening, and his face dropped. Surprisingly, I was calm, very calm. I went to my book and started repeating, "My vine shall not cast its fruit before its

Chapter 2. Happily Ever After

time." This passage spoke of miscarriage and I believed with all my heart I would not lose this baby.

I called the doctor and explained what was happening. They didn't hesitate to tell me that what I was describing at this stage in the pregnancy meant I was losing the baby. I was instructed to go to the hospital, where a dilation and curettage or D and C, a procedure to remove tissue from inside my uterus, would be performed to expand the cervix of the uterus. They said they would have liked to have given me a scan but there were no appointments available.

At that point, I could do nothing but pray. I took out my little book and started going through the scriptures. When I finished, I got into the shower; I was still bleeding but I had a calm about me because I knew I was going to be okay. This was the Jackie Mize in me, refusing to succumb to the words of the medical professionals on this one. That scan was necessary, so I put my faith out there and prayed to God to make it happen – to give me a miracle. By the time I'd finished in the shower, my mobile phone rang, and I listened to the voice on the other end of the line.

"Mrs Sillah, we've literally just had a cancellation for a scan, so if you want to make your way down to the hospital for 11:20, we'll see you then."

Relieved was not the word! Eddie and I drove down to the hospital and managed to get there on time. The sonographer and midwife spoke to me about what was happening and that this process of having an ultrasound scan was just a formality. I may need a D and C, or I may be okay. I'll never forget Eddie sitting next to me with his right leg shaking. He had his hands clasped under his chin and his face was so serious.

The next minute, I was lying down with gel spread across my belly waiting to see who was right about me losing my baby.

"Oh! The baby's there!"

I turned and looked to see this little thing kicking its arms and legs for dear life. I knew it! I just knew my baby girl was going to be all right and she was. Eddie was so relieved.

"I told you! I told you she would be all right!" I said to Eddie.

★★★

I had a beautiful pregnancy apart from that 'little' scare. I enjoyed every minute of it; I was healthy, happy and complete. We moved home in June in the fifth month of my pregnancy. It was a lovely summer that year and as I was having an easy time, I didn't let the heat get to me too much. We moved into a townhouse which has got to be the most ridiculous place to live when you're heavily pregnant. The number of times I just sat on the stairs and cried when Eddie wasn't home to go get me some cold water, because the thought of climbing those steps could have sent me into an early labour.

Eddie was great and eventually got me a mini-fridge to put in our room. We had no bed or settee because everything was on order, so comfort wasn't something I experienced much of when we first moved into our new home. I managed though.

Throughout my pregnancy I'd been working at two councils. The first was Barking and Dagenham where I left on my birthday, 11 August, to go and ironically work with Eddie again in Wandsworth Council. Exactly two weeks before my due date which was the 25 October, I gave up work.

I had bought all the baby's things. Even though I had got as far as washing, drying and laying them out, I was too tired to iron and pack the ones I needed for my hospital bag. It was time to sit and relax on the couch. Eddie was tired too so we both decided to have a quiet evening. We watched TV with me sitting on the couch and Eddie with his head on my lap. That's when I felt it!

"Eddie get up quickly!" I said, so I could rush to the bathroom as fast as I could.

This was a new couch and I would've been damned if I was going to have my waters break all over it. My timing was pretty good as I just about managed to get to the bathroom when I felt this gush. My waters had broken two weeks early and I was completely and utterly exhausted – we both were. It was late – after 10 o'clock – and we were about to go to bed. Instead we were frantically packing the case I thought I had time to finish getting ready.

***

At the maternity ward, we were met by a lovely midwife. I explained what had happened and that my contractions were about five minutes apart. I was taken to a room where I was examined and told to wait. While we were waiting, there was a lady in the adjacent room in the throes of labour, crying out in pain. At what must have been one of her contractions, we heard her scream.

"Bring the hoover! Bring the hoover!"

We looked at each other, confused. Then we realised the expectant mother must have been asking for the suction machine. We laughed so much that I could have given birth there and then.

The midwife returned and said I wasn't dilated far enough so should return home and come back in a few hours. Now as crazy as this sounds, the book I'd been reading said that one could confess how quickly the labour should be; I had been praying the experience would be nothing like the three-day trauma my son and I had gone through. I told the midwife that if I went back home, I was sure to have the baby there and no way was I going to give birth and leave my newly-decorated home with light walls and a cream-coloured leather couch like a crime scene from *CSI*. So, I politely refused but let Eddie leave so he could get some sleep; I was beyond exhausted already and we both needed a few hours of rest before the baby arrived.

After about two hours I had to use the bathroom which was quite a distance from the ward. I made this trip about three times without any of the nurses asking if I was okay. On my last return to my bed, I lay down and felt this pain but just imagined it was a big wave and after peaking, would come down. Suddenly, I felt this urge to push. I called out to the nurse and told her I wanted to push and needed some pain relief. She looked at me.

"You can't do!" she said.

"Well I do!" I said. I was so insistent that she said she would check how many centimetres I was.

"Oh my God! You're ten centimetres gone! There's no time to get you to the delivery suite. Just don't push!"

I was put on another bed and wheeled into a room where a very young-looking doctor and another midwife were waiting. Eddie had been contacted about an hour or so before but still had not arrived back at the hospital.

Chapter 2. Happily Ever After

Within about 15 minutes, I had the most gorgeous baby girl with a little pointed chin and a mass of curly black hair. As soon as I held her in my arms, in walked Mr Sillah. He was so shocked that he had missed it all, but I was taken care of so beautifully, I really hadn't missed him.

★★★

I'm glad I listened to my body and held fast to my belief that I would have a quick birth; had I returned home, I surely would have had my daughter either there or on the way back to the hospital and that would have been a real problem. Eddie was late because he had gotten lost. The fog that night was terrible, and visibility was very poor. Because we had just moved to the area, the roads were still unfamiliar, so tiredness mixed with the anxiety of trying to rush to the hospital must have had a knock-on effect on Eddie's sense of direction.

Baby and I had to stay in hospital for few days before going home to enjoy our new life. My family was now complete.

Chapter 3

Shattered Dreams

Eddie took over a month off work to stay at home with his new daughter. He was excellent with her. It helped that he could survive on little sleep because although our daughter was a good sleeper, she was not as excellent as her brother, who was sleeping through the night from time he was three months. My daughter would wake up about three times in the night and it was killing me. I would express a bottle, hand her to Eddie and banish them both to the living room so I could get some sleep. I think because I'd worked right up to my ninth month and not had the break I thought I would have, I never really had time to rest before having the baby. It was a shock to the system when Eddie had to go back to work, leaving me having to fend for myself. At least I'd had him when I needed him most during those first six weeks, so I had to put on my big-girl pants, suck it up and get on with it.

What I found particularly challenging was how late Eddie would come home from work. We lived in north London and work was all the way south in Wandsworth. His job involved a lot of driving so it wasn't as if he could sit down at a desk and work after his sometimes two-hour drive into the office. Let's not even think about his journey back home driving through rush-hour traffic. I wasn't at all happy about Eddie's job and really wanted him to find something close to home, but he had other plans and was working on those; in the meantime, he was getting more and more tired.

★★★

After a few years it all began to take its toll. I had long returned to work as a contractor, so we were both tired. I had a bad stint on one of my contracts where I was subjected to the most horrendous bullying, sexual harassment and victimisation. It took me a good while to get myself over the experience, and we both decided to take a two-week holiday to gather our thoughts and really put some effort into planning for our future. Eddie was excellent at being able to articulate his political views and I thought he would do well blogging.

We booked a two-week break in Portugal where we loved to spend the summer holidays. A whole two weeks was unusual for us because I was a contractor; we would typically go away for ten days but because we had both been through quite a lot, we thought we needed more time. We went away with our daughter and Eddie's niece who, incidentally, was also my goddaughter. We had travelled with her before and we felt it would be nice for our daughter to have the company; it was also my present to my goddaughter for Christmas and her birthday rolled into one. We were all looking forward to the holiday but had no idea what lay ahead.

We flew into Faro on our beloved easyJet flight, the only time I'll slum it on a flight – when the flight time was short. A driver

Chapter 3. Shattered Dreams

picked us up – he was to be our driver for the duration of our holiday. I only liked staying in hotels for very short trips or if I was travelling solo, because I could only take hotel food for so long. It was also awful to wake up early to eat breakfast whether hungry or not, at sometimes 7 o'clock, and for a limited time too. That was so not my idea of a holiday! For family holidays, my preference was always to book an apartment where I could cook and have control over what and when I eat. So, our typical routine would be to be picked up from the airport and driven straight to a supermarket where I would stock up on all my household essentials and as much fresh fish, king prawns, pizzas and other foods I know my brood would want to eat.

We'd booked a lovely apartment with a wonderful landlady. It really was a home from home, with everything needed to make our stay comfortable. It was in the Algarve, right near the marina. That area was particularly beautiful at night, especially walking along the marina with the lights shining across the water and people out having a good time, eating ice cream, drinking cocktails and listening to the bad singing from one of the popular karaoke bars. It was a lovely, warm and peaceful place to be and we adored being there.

I'd told all of three of them I was doing absolutely nothing for the first three days, so wasn't expecting any whining and whingeing about going out. I knew that out of the 14 days we were going to be there, that would be the only time I would have to rest.

I got my wish and managed to keep the crew under control until day four. Both the girls were eager to visit the water park, which was some way from the apartment. We all got ready to enjoy a day out in the beautiful Algarve sun. Our driver was dead on time to collect us at 1 o'clock to begin the hour-long journey. We had one stop to make to buy tickets. When we got to the ticket stall, much to the girls' disappointment, we had left home too late to get our hands on any tickets; to say they were upset is an understatement. Nobody can express disappointment like the younger Miss Sillah and boy was she upset. As a compromise, as the beach wasn't too far away, I managed to convince the girls that we would do the water park the following day but could have a nice lunch at the beach and a splash in the sea. I must have been convincing because the conversation immediately turned to what we were going to eat and where. We found a nice restaurant with outside seating, a table for four looking out to the very blue sea was secured and we ordered something to eat.

While waiting for our food to arrive, we decided to take some pictures. The girls did their usual crazy poses, and Eddie decided he wanted me to take some pictures of him. We took a few 'selfies', and I took some of Eddie on his own. I showed him the pictures and he pulled a face before complaining he didn't like how he looked. Now if Eddie ever took pictures of me and I dared to complain about how I looked, I would be met by his standard response.

"I'm a photographer, not a magician!"

So, I couldn't resist saying it right back at him, especially as he was asking for it, but something made me cut my laughter short when I heard the tone of his voice.

"My face looks funny. I don't like how my face looks," he said.

I looked at the pictures and back at my husband.

Chapter 3. Shattered Dreams

"My face looks funny," he said again, and took a slow sip of water. "My water tastes funny as well. I feel like I'm coming 'round from an anaesthetic."

I was uneasy. Eddie's face had dropped on one side and I immediately thought he was having a stroke. The driver had left us, so we had no means of getting back to the apartment quickly and I needed to get him some help – fast. He was calm. His words were not slurred, nor did he have any of the symptoms you associate with a stroke.

I didn't panic either and said I would call our doctor in London for advice. When I was out of sight, tears rolled down my face. In my heart I knew that whatever it was, it was serious because those tears had been involuntarily. By nature, I didn't panic; I took care of business and fell apart later if I needed to, but I just knew this was different. I didn't let Eddie or the girls see me cry as I had composed myself by the time I returned to our table.

"The doctor said to get to the hospital as soon as we can," I told Eddie.

The driver came back for us. As God would have it, our apartment was directly opposite a private clinic. When we arrived back at the apartment and after offloading our things, I went across the road to the clinic for an appointment. Eddie hadn't raised any objections, which was unlike him. Things were serious.

***

When I got to the reception desk, that's when my worry manifested. I spoke at a hundred words a minute about how I needed my husband to be seen because he might be having a stroke and blah, blah, blah. I just needed them to hear he needed help *immediately*, that he was across the road, and could I bring him in straightaway. The lady was lovely. She told me they were due to close in ten minutes but would wait for me to come back. The apartment was literally across the road from the clinic, but by the time I walked through the front door I was calm and completely composed.

"Eddie. They said the doctor can see you, so let's go."

He didn't say a word but just simply got up from the small dining table in the corner of the room. Within a few minutes we were back at the clinic in the doctor's office. Eddie's face had improved somewhat but there was still a slight droop on the left side. His speech was fine and he was calm but I could see he was worried.

"How long have you been feeling like this?" the doctor asked.

I answered for Eddie and explained it had been about three hours. The doctor asked if he'd been under any unusual stress or was worried about anything. Eddie said he hadn't been. The doctor then examined him on the hospital bed. After the examination and a series of questions about his lifestyle and what had happened that afternoon, he was given two aspirin tablets. The doctor then told us Eddie had had a stroke. A note was given to us to see a Dr Romero at a private hospital near the airport with strict instructions to be seen immediately.

★★★

Our driver drove us straight to the hospital. On arrival we passed on the note to the receptionist. After a short wait, we were called into another room with Dr Romero. Another examination took place confirming the initial diagnosis. They were optimistic because we'd acted quickly, he'd had aspirin already and all this improved his chances of recovery. More aspirin was given, and a flurry of doctors and nurses kept popping in and out from behind the curtains that were drawn around Eddie's bed.

By this time is it was gone 9 o'clock at night and I was worried about the girls who we'd left in the apartment on their own. Finally, the doctor in charge said my husband would be home in about three or four days after further observation. I eventually left the hospital and went back to the girls. I had no idea that that day, 28 August 2015, was going to change my life forever…

★★★

The next day, the doctors informed me that an MRI scan of Eddie's brain had been done; there were no signs of a stroke, so they were baffled by the facial paralysis. Initially they thought it may have been Bell's palsy which can cause weakness or a total loss of muscle usage control. One of the main reasons this was ruled out in the end was because with some facial massage from the physiotherapist, his face had already practically returned to normal by the third day.

On that third day, I received a phone call from my husband in the morning saying he had seen a nurse and someone else and they'd asked that I come to the hospital as soon as possible. He'd had some tests and the nurse had given him the thumbs up on all of them except one.

"Her face just went funny and she said to talk to the doctor. She didn't really say anything after that," Eddie said.

I was perplexed. I had a quick shower and left for the hospital. When I arrived, I was met by a doctor, a neurologist and a neurosurgeon in Eddie's room.

"Did your husband walk into this hospital on his own?" the neurosurgeon asked.

"Yes, he did," I answered, though confused. The question was asked again, as if I had misheard the first time. I responded just as emphatically, adding I would know if I had a six-foot-two-inch man mountain on my back.

What was said to us after that stunned and shocked us. Eddie could not leave the hospital because any sudden movement could lead to paralysis from the neck down or cause a blood clot to the brain. They'd found an undetected compression on his spinal cord that could sever the cord at any time, so they had to operate immediately to relieve the pressure. It was an exceptionally delicate and painful operation we were told but as he was fit and healthy, the recovery time was around five days. By that time, he would be able to tie his own shoelaces and should make a full recovery.

We couldn't believe what we were hearing. Here was my husband who had never so much as spent one night in a hospital being told he risked death or paralysis from the neck down. Just like that. It was surreal. He was scared and so was I. It was time to think about consent for the operation, but to be honest, did we really have any choice? Did we need to think about it? We were 'ambushed' by three people and advised by one of the top surgeons in Portugal. Who were we to disagree?

So, Eddie consented, and the ball started rolling. As his blood had thinned after a few days of aspirin, it needed time to recover before he had an operation; thin blood would

Chapter 3. Shattered Dreams

increase the risk of haemorrhage. That reversal of the aspirin effect would take a minimum of five days.

It was tough on the girls. Our daughter accused me of lying to her that her father would be coming back home shortly to enjoy the rest of our holiday. The poor child was only eight, so it was a challenge to keep coming home without her father. We had to explain to her that she needed to go back to England because Daddy wasn't well enough to come home. Our son had to come and get the girls and fly them back to London. Little did I know that apart from the one I was facing with my husband's illness, I had another battle to fight.

Chapter 4

The Battle

When Eddie and I first walked into hospital, we were immediately asked if we had insurance. Thankfully we did and that was why we were fortunate enough to be able to go to one of Faro's top private hospitals. I had to surrender a credit card in the interim. Now that it was established that he was not going to be discharged as was initially thought, the process of applying for insurance began.

I called the insurance company and told them what was going on. Initially they were supportive until I had to speak to an officer in the medical team. Again, I explained in detail what had happened to my husband, why he couldn't fly and the fact that he needed emergency surgery. The medical team would discuss the case and then get back to me. I waited a whole day for their call, and when it eventually came, it wasn't good news.

"Mrs Sillah, we've discussed your husband's case and we would like to fly him back to London to be assessed."

I asked the woman on the other end of the phone to explain what she meant by that as Eddie had already been assessed by a doctor, neurologist and a neurosurgeon at one of the best hospitals in Portugal. A decision had been made and a prognosis given, so what was there to assess? All she said was that the decision had been made. I was not having it. I asked her why they would not take the word of not one, not two but three doctors and surgeons from a hospital that they had approved. Did they have no confidence in the hospital?

"Please get off the phone and don't call me until you and your so-called medical team can answer that question because I am not having anyone mess with my husband's health," I retorted. "God forbid if anything happens to my husband because of your nonsense. There will be hell to pay for. You have until 10 o'clock to call me back with an answer."

By 9:50 she'd called back. "Hello Mrs Sillah. If you insist, we'll authorise the operation". Just as well, as it was time for Eddie to proceed.

I wasn't relieved but bloody mad at the audacity, cheek and sheer insensitivity of this 'computer says no' character. "Now if you could get your finger out and get my son to take my girls back home, I would be grateful. Being here waiting for this call means I'm being delayed from going to the hospital and I really don't appreciate that."

I got myself and the children together to see Eddie and give him the news. He was relieved. We'd spoken about going back to England but we both knew that he was in the best place. It wasn't safe to fly, and we put our trust in the decision that had already been made for us.

★★★

Chapter 4. The Battle

Our son flew in to collect the girls but was only able to spend a day with us. I was relieved in a way because it was way too hard to put on a brave face for everyone. When under pressure, I functioned better alone. Soon it was just Eddie and I but all I could think of was the empty two-bedroom apartment that was supposed to be filled with the laughter of children running around, bringing wet feet into the house, and our chatter as we ate lunch on the terrace with Eddie and I on the couch watching a movie with me sipping champagne whilst the girls were in bed. How could so much change so quickly? I consoled myself knowing that in approximately two weeks, my husband would be out of the hospital and we would be on our way home.

I made the daily trips to see Eddie. It was quite some distance from our apartment but that didn't matter. However, it was expensive as I had to use the driver to get there – public transport on that route was practically non-existent.

It cost 50 euros a day but fortunately, the driver being quite upset at our fate, reduced the cost by 10 euros for me; I was grateful.

The operation was scheduled for 10 September 2015. The day before, for the first time in my life, I remained awake for 24 hours. After coming back from visiting Eddie, I couldn't eat or sleep. I just paced my room until morning when the driver came to pick me up. I was immensely anxious about it all but had to be calm and a pillar for Eddie because I knew he was scared and that saddened me. The operation was due at 9:30 that morning and I was there nearly an hour earlier. We chatted and prayed together, asking God to bring him out of the surgery and to have all that was wrong with him put right. I was hopeful because after all there must have been a reason why he wasn't paralysed and hadn't suffered a clot to the brain as we were told might happen. So, I decided to be the woman of faith I had always been and remained calm. Finally, Eddie was prepped and taken to theatre for the two-hour procedure.

I sat in the big, black leather reclining chair where I finally fell asleep. When I woke up, I realised I'd been asleep for only an hour and a half. *Only 30 more minutes* I thought to myself. However, it was another hour and a half before the surgeon came and told me that the operation had been successful but that they had put him in the intensive care unit. I managed to find the strength to sigh a sigh of relief and crack a brief smile. I gently muttered under my breath after thanking the surgeon, 'Thank you Jesus'.

It was a little while before I was able to see him. When I did, he smiled that Eddie smile and I cannot tell you how good it felt to see it. The surgeon came 'round to brief us on what to expect in the following days and it all seemed straightforward. They were happy with the surgery and how he was responding; it was all going great. Then two days later Eddie became unwell.

He'd contracted an infection in the wound and all hell broke loose from that point. This was where the story changed for us completely. Eddie went from making great progress to going downhill…fast. He was put on high dosages of antibiotics, painkillers, you name it – but nothing seemed to work. He made a full turn from walking and doing all that he was used to doing, to having to be cared for around the clock.

Chapter 4. The Battle

I went to the hospital first thing in the morning to bathe him, brush his teeth and try and feed him. I say try because he refused to eat. In the end he lost over 30 pounds in the space of two weeks. I was beside myself. This was not supposed to happen. How did we get here? I had no clue, but I constantly prayed it would end. I was reassured that the infection would clear, and Eddie could come home to the apartment but would have to stay in Portugal for a week before going home.

By this time, we'd been in the holiday apartment for nearly a month, but fortunately the insurance company told me we could move to another one. I couldn't find a one-bedroom property up to the standard we were used to and as the price difference was not that great, they agreed to us moving to a lovely two-bedroom property in one of the nicest hotels in the Algarve. The hospital had to explain to the insurers that as my husband was so unwell, getting to the main hotel for meals would not be feasible so a self-contained place would be easier for us.

Everything seemed fine with the insurance company. I had a lovely officer who was very reassuring and didn't give me too much grief when I had to call them to give updates on Eddie's condition and stay. However, it wasn't long before it became evident that Eddie's situation was getting worse and our departure would be delayed. Eventually I was told that I couldn't care for him outside of the hospital. It was hard. It was really hard. The goal posts kept changing constantly and each time we both had to take it on the chin and remain in faith and optimism. I'll never forget when my husband looked into my eyes in excruciating pain and said, "My life is in your hands." That's the level of trust and confidence he had in the woman he'd married, and I wasn't going to let him down. I knew that whatever happened, I had to take him back to his children. There was no way I would return to London without their father. Now just before our holiday, I'd secured a new contract but now had to inform my bosses of what was going on. They allowed me to work remotely for a couple of weeks but that became more and more challenging, so I lost the job. To be honest, it was a relief. I know we needed to keep up with bills but I needed to give my full attention to Eddie.

When it became clear to the insurance company that Eddie would have to stay in hospital in Portugal, the real battle began. The whole thing was expensive; he was in a private hospital and I was in a five-star hotel apartment with meals. To be honest, I hardly ate much – just in the evenings and a few mojitos which I felt I deserved under the circumstances. There was one saving grace from the battle. Word had gone around about my fate and the Portuguese staff took me under their wing – from the bartenders, to the waiters and waitresses, to the concierge and receptionists. A lovely young girl from Belarus offered to take me to the hospital on the days she wasn't working. The landlady of the first apartment we'd stayed in at the start of this ill-fated holiday was Persian and lived in Ireland. She travelled to Portugal regularly as it was her second home. Had it not been that she had other guests booked to stay at the apartment, she'd wanted me to stay there, free of charge. I was astounded. On two occasions she and her husband took me out to dinner to cheer me up. This journey I was on wasn't easy, but my God, many angels were put in my path to hold me up during those months.

Chapter 4. The Battle

And then there was the insurance company. They'd made it crystal clear from the outset that they didn't want Eddie to remain in Portugal. It wasn't as if we wanted to stay for the hell of it; it was just the best thing for him. They rang often to ask me the status of my husband's stay and not his health. They were fully aware of how ill he was and were given strict instructions to call me but on more than one occasion, they called to subtly bully him to claim he was well enough to be flown back to London. His was now a secondary matter for them and all they cared about was how much money we were costing them; obviously we had planned the whole thing and would rather be holed up in a hospital, spending 50 euros a day as opposed to being in our apartment in good health and good company. They were so mercenary in the way they handled us. Their main objective was to fly us back to London and we had no issue with that. What we were unhappy about was in their quest to return us back to British soil, my husband's health ceased to be a priority and that couldn't work for me. This was my husband, father to my children and I was not going to have him dealt with as a faceless case number. He had people who loved and cared about him and wanted to see him well. There was an eight-year-old child waiting for me to bring her Daddy back…this was my life they were being so blasé about and I was not going to take it. Eddie's words, 'My life is in your hand,' meant I had to do right by him; he was relying on me.

***

The medical staff at the hospital were amazing though. Eddie had always been able to charm everyone around him.

If it wasn't the smile, it was the monumental amount of knowledge he would share with everyone he met. As sick as he was, he never missed an opportunity to chat in depth with his nurses and doctors. The surgeon who had been looking after Eddie was a bespectacled man in his 50s with grey and black hair. He was supportive and knowledgeable from the get-go and knowing that he was one of the best surgeons in Portugal really helped us in the early days.

He always explained everything to us in intricate detail and was just there for us.

At this point, Eddie developed a high fever so was being monitored closely. Within a few hours the insurance company had called me to say they had contacted the surgeon and had been advised that we could now return to a medical facility in London as my husband was fit to fly. I knew that could not be possible because Eddie had taken such a turn for the worse. There was just no way he could be certified fit to fly. My caseworker had now changed and we were lumbered with a horrible and obnoxious woman who had clearly resorted to lying. The caseworker sneakily spoke to a doctor who was involved in Eddie's care and claimed that he had given the go ahead for a flight to take us back to London. They actually expected to put my husband on a normal flight with him lying across seats. It would have been funny if they weren't serious. I was furious. I didn't need the added stress, but I realised I wasn't dealing with normal people. All I knew was that I had been trusted to deal with Eddie's affairs, so I just flew into action.

I spoke to the surgeon and he confirmed, as I thought, that no such instruction was given. Their priority was to stabilize him and then take it from there. One of the key decisions that had been made was that Eddie needed to be in a neuro-rehabilitation centre, or a hospital that had those facilities otherwise he ran the risk or regressing, reducing his chances of a full recovery. I was not about to let that happen. The surgeon was so good to us. He reassured me that we had his full support and he would do all that he could to ensure that Eddie stayed with them for as long as was medically necessary.

It continued to be a hellish ordeal dealing with the insurers. I explained to them, as did the doctors, that it was imperative that Eddie went straight into a hospital specialising in neurology back in London. We were told that he would have to go to one of the local hospitals before he could be transferred. The problem with that was there was no time; time was precious and any lost not having the neurological physiotherapy could seriously hamper his chances of returning to what was a normal life for him. I then took it upon myself to ring a few doctor friends of mine to find out where would be the best place for Eddie to go. They recommended UCLH but it was clear from what they told me that he would still have to go through a local hospital. They did give me the name of a neurosurgeon in UCLH who was apparently very good and could possibly help me. So, I called the hospital to see if I could to speak to her.

***

A lovely receptionist picked up the phone. I calmly explained I was ringing from Portugal and recounted what had been going on; I could hear from her voice that she empathised.

Although she couldn't put the call through to the surgeon, she said she would pass on a message for her to call me back. That was no good to me because I had to speak to her straight away.

The receptionist said the surgeon was going into theatre and was likely to be a few hours and it was already 9 o'clock at night. I had had little sleep, little food and was emotionally drained. I think she sensed my desperation and determination so she promised she would personally ensure I spoke to the surgeon. I kept calling and eventually got through to the surgeon at 3 o'clock the following morning. I had sat up for six hours; how could I sleep? It was worth the wait as she was amazing. She listened. She cared. She asked me to send whatever medical information I had on my husband for her to give me her opinion and get some indication of what was needed.

***

The following day, the insurance company, eager to show their power, sent me a letter at 5 o'clock on a Friday afternoon to tell me an air ambulance had been arranged to bring Eddie and I back to London, claiming there was no reason for us to remain on Portuguese soil. They believed they had fulfilled their legal obligation to have Eddie transferred to a suitable medical facility in London. I disagreed. The insurance company's version of 'suitable' and mine were very, very different. I had the backing of the surgeon who was very clear about why it was important that this part of Eddie's care and the move was executed precisely as he had stated.

So, receiving a letter at the close of business on a Friday was an underhanded move to force us to travel, knowing full

Chapter 4. The Battle

well it was putting Eddie at risk. The surgeon contacted the insurance company to explain the position, but I had received 'proof' he had authorised Eddie's release from hospital; again, this was false because no release had been granted by the person who was looking after my husband. The insurance company said they were no longer paying for my room or Eddie's medical care. We were on our own. They contacted the hotel to let them know that I was to vacate the room as they wouldn't be paying after that day. I remember sitting on the couch in the apartment, hungry, wanting to eat, yearning to go see my husband but not being able to do either. If I left the room, I wouldn't be able to return. I had to drink endless cups of warm water to stave off the hunger. The staff continued to be nice to me – they didn't even try to make me leave even though the clock was ticking.

I had managed to get my lawyer who was excellent in the nick of time. She eventually got the insurance company to back down especially as the surgeon disputed that he had written a letter of release for his patient. We had a little more time and every day Eddie was cared for in that facility was an extra day that gave me hope.

Chapter 5

Return to Base

The battle had ensued for a long time. I had done all I could do and the medical staff though not happy, were also tired. We agreed to go home and hope for the best. Truth be told, we were eager to get back for our daughter's ninth birthday on 13 October, so when we were told that this was the date we were leaving, I was relieved.

We flew back via air ambulance with two nurses and a doctor. Eddie was in such pain that his medication had to be constantly topped up. I just wanted him comfortable and safe. The flight was smooth enough, but it felt strange being in such a small aircraft. I guess it was because I'd always thought if I was ever in a small plane it would be a private jet because I had finally made it in life…not an air ambulance. This was not quite what I had in mind. The plane landed at an airbase in Letchworth in the early evening and we were then transferred to an ambulance bound for North Middlesex Hospital. Finally, we were home.

★★★

I hadn't told our daughter we'd be back for her birthday. I really didn't know what was going on and the way things changed from one minute to the next, the last thing I wanted to do was get her hopes up and disappoint her on her birthday. I was just grateful I was bringing her daddy home as I had promised and of course, all good mummies keep their promises.

Eddie was exhausted. It had been a gruelling journey for him. He was still not eating well so all he had eaten that day was a tiny bit of porridge in the morning and a few nibbles of some biscuits on the flight. As tired as he was, his face lit up on seeing the children. My daughter was so tired and a bit confused as to why she was going to this hospital. Her brother had kept it a secret from her too and it was only when she saw me in the corner of the room and then her dad that she realised why she was there. I got the most amazing hug from her and I just whispered in her ear, "I told you I'd bring your Daddy home."

She rushed over to Eddie but had to be stopped in her tracks. We gently explained that Daddy was in a lot of pain and because of his neck, she couldn't squeeze him. She gently laid her head on his chest and rested there for a while; we all looked at each other with relief on our faces. We didn't need to say much; we knew how blessed we were to witness the picture before us.

I left the family with Eddie and spoke to the doctors. The doctor who had flown with us on the plane needed to do a detailed handover and I wanted to make sure I was present. I had arranged with the hospital to place all of Eddie's medical notes on a disc for North Middlesex to view in detail, and all that had been done. I didn't want any confusion and from the little experience I'd had with the insurance company, I didn't want anything to fall through the cracks. It was agreed that an assessment of his needs would be carried out and if a move was required, he would be sent to UCLH.

★★★

Eddie was in North Middlesex for about four weeks in the end. I visited every day to see him and to take him food. He flat out refused to eat hospital food and to be honest, you couldn't blame him. It was exhausting travelling to the hospital, taking care of the house, working, supporting victims of rape, child abuse and domestic violence through my organisation, and whatever else I needed to do, but I had to do it. It was like doing something for an extension of myself; if I fought for Eddie, I fought for me. I couldn't imagine it being any other way in my head or, indeed my heart. I knew it wouldn't be for long because Eddie was going to get better and things would go back to normal. These thoughts would always be followed by a prayer of thanksgiving under my breath, "Thank you Lord for not making me a widow."

During Eddie's stay at North Middlesex, I expressed my concern about his lack of exercise. He literally lay in his bed for days on end because they didn't have the facilities needed for his care; this was the precise reason for the fight I had put up with the insurance company. We knew his condition would deteriorate if the right medical attention wasn't given. This really started to demoralise Eddie and it worried me too. The one thing that kept him going was the fact that I would always advocate for him no matter what. It was obvious why the insurance company were eager to get rid of us; we learnt that the total bill for Eddie's care was within the region of 75,000 euros – amazing how much a life of a loved one is worth these days! Finally, the move to UCLH was agreed – what a relief! The move was to ensure his specialised care and to thoroughly investigate what his neurological needs were. We thought we were finally where we could be heard and receive help, but that feeling was short-lived.

The transfer was smooth, and Eddie settled in well. However, he was still in significant pain and as a result he could do little for himself. We had placed so much hope in his move to UCLH, so we didn't envision anything going wrong at this point. One morning, Eddie was due to have a procedure for his pain relief. He was being given drugs intravenously through a line which now had to be removed. He was told he would be collected via ambulance in the morning, at about 8 o'clock, to be transferred to another department on the UCLH campus for the procedure. The ambulance arrived on time, picked Eddie up but had him down as someone else! I was livid when I arrived to find this out. How could that possibly have happened? Patients had to confirm their name and date of birth countless times to whoever asked to avoid situations like this; one thing was for sure, this was not a good start! Eventually though he got where he needed to be.

During his stay, he was seen by the registrar and a consultant. After his assessment, it was decided that he could be discharged. I remember him calling me, very distressed and not understanding how or why such a decision could be made as he hadn't really had the care we were expecting. I was exceptionally angry because all medical staff from Portugal to London knew that no decisions were to be taken without my knowledge or involvement. It baffled me as to why on

Chapter 5. Return to Base

such a crucial matter as a discharge from hospital, having had major surgery that had gone wrong, they had excluded the very person he would be discharged to. I asked for a meeting with the registrar who had made the decision and asked how a man who was so ill, bed-ridden and needing 24-hour care could be marked for discharge with no discussion, plan or support in place. Were they aware of our living arrangements, our family situation or our financial situation for that matter? I told them what they were doing was forcing a man to live a life of permanent disability when he didn't need to.

For a once-proud, strong, independent man, this was soul-destroying and devastating mentally, emotionally and financially for the family, especially me. I was the one who would bear the brunt of that decision aside from Eddie himself of course. I refused to take him home; simple as that. I refused to take him home for him to be discarded as if he didn't matter. "My life is in your hands," he'd told me, and I wasn't ready nor was I prepared to wash my husband off my hands. That's not how it worked for me. I challenged them to give him what they knew he needed, and that was to get him the neurological rehabilitation he desperately required.

I remember writing a letter of complaint about my husband's care that wasn't even acknowledged, though finally I got what I wanted for Eddie. They had to transfer him back to North Middlesex Hospital, but they agreed they would place him in the Edgware Neuro-Rehabilitation Centre; after a few weeks he was transferred there where he finally began his rehab. As the funding for the placement at the rehab centre didn't come from our local borough, I was informed he could only stay for four weeks. The rehab centre was good for him because the programme was intense, structured and carried out by specialists who knew what he needed to improve his mobility.

Within a short time, we could see improvements. He started with a Zimmer frame, then progressed to crutches; this was a huge achievement for him but bittersweet at the same time. Eddie was supposed to be going to work, doing the things he loved like watching the news and football in the comfort of his own home, playing with his daughter and being a husband to me. Instead he was in this place learning how to walk again. I felt the injustice of it all. Life really was unfair and I often struggled to make sense of what was going on.

It was hard on the family to have Eddie placed in Edgware, even though that was the best place for him. The distance was taking its toll on me, as it was an hour-plus on public transport and a fifteen-minute walk from the station. By this time, it was December 2015 and I had done four months of going from one hospital to another to look after my husband and fight if I had to, to ensure he was getting the best care possible. I don't think I let myself appreciate how exhausted I actually was, especially as I had to also look for paid work aside from the support work I was doing with women and children to provide for the family during this time.

Ten days before Christmas, I managed to find an excellent contract with the NHS. I had been worried about what kind of Christmas our daughter would have. It was tough on her, having both parents away for so long with no preparation or warning of what was going to happen. Often, I would find her crying because she didn't like to see her 'Papa' in pain. He was her hero, her protector and her knight in shining armour; a man who stood over six feet tall, was fiercely independent, immaculate in his dressing and always smelt delicious. It was so hard for her to see him so dependent.

It was important we were together as a family as often as we could, so I sought permission from the hospital to have Eddie come home to us for Christmas. They agreed that it was possible but for no more than three days. We were elated because since August, we hadn't spent a single night together. To say we were excited was an understatement; it was good for Eddie to come home and be where he belonged. My only fear was how he would feel having to go back to the centre after spending time with the family.

★★★

Christmas was a very low-key family affair. We did the normal Christmas thing for us. Breakfast was always smoked salmon and cream cheese bagels with scrambled eggs and champagne. Eddie didn't really like turkey so there was always either a roast beef or nicely seasoned roast lamb; this Christmas was special, so we had both with all the trimmings. Apple crumble was on the menu, with cream of course, but Eddie loved, and I mean loved, custard and ice cream and somehow managed both with his dessert. It was lovely to see him happy and eating good food. He loathed the food at the centre so I had to make sure he had food he could eat during the week when I was at work. That meant I would cook over the weekends. Sure enough, three days later, Eddie returned to rehab. Now that we'd had a taster of being together after so long, we were looking forward to when he finally came home for good.

Everything was going well until I received a phone call from the centre saying Eddie had had a bad fall. He had been going for dinner when he lost his balance and fallen backwards and blacked out. An ambulance had taken him to Barnet General Hospital. I was in a state of shock when I got that phone call and then just started to cry. It seemed like any progress we made was taken from us in an instant. How much could one man suffer? I know I couldn't take much more so only God knew how my husband was feeling.

Eddie was told he didn't need to stay in hospital overnight so could go back to the centre; they had run some tests which were all okay, meaning he could be discharged at some point during the evening. When I spoke to him, he seemed drowsy and tired but reassured me that he was okay which was all I needed to hear. It turned out that he had fallen much earlier than when I'd received the call. I was upset I had not been called immediately but the way events had unfolded meant I had to wait until the following day to see him. No one was sure what time he would be discharged, and I could well pass them on my way to the hospital while they were on their way back to the centre. I was coming all the way from south London too so it was likely I would miss them.

Even though he'd had the fall, Eddie was due to be discharged from the centre just after Christmas. How could that be if he had sustained a serious fall and experienced such a setback? There was a lot of to-ing and fro-ing and eventually, they agreed to keep him for an extra week. We were all left disappointed that it couldn't be longer; though we wanted him home, we wanted him home fit. This was yet another hurdle Eddie had to climb but he was tough and proud and wasn't about to give up the fight. So, he soldiered on as the warrior he was.

Chapter 6

Home Sweet Home

His return home was much anticipated, and we began to look forward to the future. There was a lot of physiotherapy for Eddie to get through – that we weren't naïve about. As we lived in a house with three floors, it was best to convert our living room so that he could use the bathroom which was only next door. We had aids installed to help him get in and out of the bath and make it easier for him to use the toilet. With everything within relatively easy reach, it went some way to restoring a level of the independence he had lost over the last nearly six months.

I still had to work and as much as I would have liked to have been a full-time carer for Eddie, he would have hated that, and we simply couldn't afford it. I managed by being super-organised in getting him his breakfast before leaving for work, something ready to eat for lunch and then coming home straight from work to serve him dinner. It worked for us and we did fall into a routine; maybe not what we were used to, but it was our new, temporary normal. Work was full-time, so was my charity and activism work as was motherhood and being a wife. I had to wear many hats and keep all the plates spinning basically because there wasn't really anyone to pass those plates on to.

It baffled people when they found out my husband was still unwell. When it had all started in Portugal, I had to publicly declare Eddie's illness. This was mostly driven by the fact that I'd planned a charity ball for October 2015 but at the time we had no idea we wouldn't be back in London. A lot of time was spent deliberating what I was going to do and was under immense pressure, stressing about what I would say. Tickets had already been bought by some of our supporters but most of all, I knew Eddie didn't want anyone to know that he was sick.

In the end I decided to put out a statement on my social media handles advising people that my husband was ill and that I couldn't get back to London to hold the ball. I was really between a rock and a hard place but decided the wrath of Eddie was better and easier to manage than the public thinking the first event I was holding was not genuine. I can't express how relieved I felt once that statement went out – as uncomfortable as it was for me, it took the pressure off somewhat. I never went back on social media to update anyone on my husband's progress, not just because he wouldn't have liked it, but to be honest, it was our business and we were still coming to terms with everything.

The contracting work I relied on to a degree to help support the family was becoming harder to secure. The market was steadily changing so I had to look at what I could do to support my family and still pursue my own dreams. I threw myself

Chapter 6. Home Sweet Home

into supporting and coaching people, especially women, and because of what I was going through I think it gave me a deeper sense of the challenges people faced that nobody really knew about. It gave me first-hand insight into how the whole world could seem to be against you, and yet you slap on your make-up, go to work and be a boss, attend parents' evenings, support a woman 5,000 miles away who has been sexually assaulted and needs emotional support, socialise and all the rest, and then come home and at times break down and wonder how you're going to pay a bill or meet a deadline. Nobody knows, because you don't complain, and you don't wish upon a star that things were different. You become very aware things are no longer the same and have changed in the way you'd not anticipated or wanted but you deal with it because too many people look up to you and rely on you for you to crumble. So, you go to bed when you can, but maybe your sleep is not the best because though the body may appear to be resting, the mind is active. You realise you've only managed less than five hours' sleep. Nevertheless, you get out of bed and do it all over again because the brightness of your 'Good morning everyone' is what they rely on to get through their day.

★★★

After Eddie had been home for a couple of months, the painkillers were now being reduced. He had been in excruciating pain since the operation in hospital but, in addition to that, he had sustained first-degree burns to his back while in Portugal. One day, he'd been in so much pain that he'd asked for a hot water bottle to help give him some relief. Somehow it burst and left him with these burns, so in addition to healing from the main operation, Eddie had this hurdle to get over as well.

As he was being weaned off the pain medication he started to complain of a pain in his groin. A senior physiotherapist came home to assess him and said she suspected he had arthritis in his hip. We were told it was very possible it was coincidental but that they would investigate more. X-rays were done which confirmed the diagnosis and it was likely that this contributed to the delay in an improvement in his mobility. The pain had become progressively worse and would make Eddie fall if he wasn't supported. His stubbornness and independence didn't help because a few times I caught him going to the bathroom without crutches and just about able to get back to the living room without falling. While I was about to have a heart attack when he did that, he would proudly tell me how well he was doing and for me to watch him walk unaided!

★★★

I will never forget Christmas 2016. We were spending the holiday with one of my sisters and had driven there a few days before Christmas Day to spend some time with her family. On Christmas Eve, we were having a merry old time prepping the spread for the following day, drinking my favourite drink, Kir Royale and playing music. Eddie had gone up to bed and I had stayed up until about 2 o'clock in the morning. When I eventually climbed into bed where he was sleeping soundly, I was a little worse for wear so got into bed as quietly as I could without waking him. I had probably been asleep for a couple of hours when something made me open my eyes. In the dark,

Chapter 6. Home Sweet Home

I couldn't see Eddie in bed; I blinked a couple of times to get my eyes to readjust to the dark and to get my tipsy head to focus. I could just about make Eddie out, kneeling beside the bed with this elbows and head resting where he should have been lying.

"Eddie! What are you doing at the side of the bed? Are you okay?"

"I think I might have broken my ankle. I was going to the toilet and I fell in the bathroom. I didn't want to wake you up."

"What?! You didn't want to wake me?! So, you've been here in pain watching me sleep?! Are you crazy? I've got to call an ambulance!"

To say I was upset was a gross understatement. I was so… well…upset that my husband had a fall without me knowing. It's bad enough to think he had broken his ankle and I was in la-la land but knowing he had been in pain for so long really hurt my heart. I was also very angry because I'd had a conversation with Eddie telling him we were not in our house so to make sure he used his crutches, no matter how short the distance; under no circumstances was he to use the bathroom or any other room without them. But did he listen? No! After all, I was only the wife!

I called the ambulance and thankfully they arrived quickly. They came up the stairs to the room, just as I had managed to get dressed. About two ambulance staff got him down the stairs and into the ambulance around 5 o'clock. Looking at the angle of his foot in relation to his ankle, there was no doubt Eddie's ankle was broken – it was truly horrendous.

We were in casualty for eight hours on Christmas Day. I was so looking forward to the day that I couldn't believe something so totally out of the blue had ruined it for Eddie. The doctor that saw us said the break was a very bad one, so much so that a metal pin would have to be inserted otherwise the bones wouldn't set properly. This meant surgery which they wanted booked in as soon as possible. How soon? By the 4 January soon.

We returned home to make the most of what was left of our Christmas with the family after Eddie had his ankle put in a temporary cast. I had to dig deep on this one. Before the fall, Eddie was on crutches and had managed a level of independence. This had relieved some of the responsibility of caring for him to some extent. In the twinkling of an eye, we had taken ten steps back, no pun intended, because now he wouldn't be able to walk at all. He was in a non-weight bearing cast and this meant that he would need 24-hour care and support.

We managed to get to the day of the operation with my heart in my mouth, as usual, because I didn't want to have to be the one on the other side of the curtain pacing up and down, looking at the clock, not knowing when they would come out of theatre. Thankfully, everything went well and Eddie, after spending a couple of days in hospital, was discharged.

***

Six weeks passed and when the time came for the cast to come off, the consultant and doctors were very happy with the way he had healed. One thing that the doctors were surprised about was the way the ankle had broken. They asked if there was any history of bone disease or arthritis within the family but there was none that Eddie knew of. He mentioned to them

Chapter 6. Home Sweet Home

that he fell because of the pain in his hip. The doctors, armed with this information, wrote to the GP so further investigations could be done. After a lot of back and forth, it was confirmed that Eddie did indeed have arthritis, that the bone in his hip had collapsed and was the cause of the excruciating pain in his groin. After a couple of appointments with an excellent consultant, it was agreed the only way to solve the problem would be to replace the hip.

The time between the diagnosis and the operation was hell for Eddie. He was in agonising pain and even though he used pain relief patches and morphine to manage it, nothing seemed to give him any meaningful relief. His quality of life began to deteriorate rapidly. He couldn't sleep and having neighbours who were so grossly inconsiderate with their music, playing it loudly at odd times, made it even harder for him to rest. I know the constant pain was having a horrible effect on him and we both couldn't wish for a date for the operation to come through quick enough. Eventually, we got our long-awaited letter. The operation was scheduled for October 2018 and we couldn't wait.

Eddie was more than excited and for the first time in three years, he could honestly see the light at the end of the tunnel. This was the first time he had really let himself go and began to plan what he was going to do with his future. He always said, "Dilys, if I can just get rid of this pain, man, I will be able to do my thing."

I knew he was of course going to be fine and I was in fact, super-optimistic. I started planning Christmas again in my head and thought this was going to be a big one. Having Eddie standing on his feet, pain-free and without any walking aids would be a dream come true for me and I let my imagination run wild on how we were going to start to really enjoy life again. We'd already started talking about downsizing and moving outside London. Eddie was addicted to property programmes and had a file on all the things he saw and liked for this new house we were going to build. We had agreed a few years before that we didn't want to buy another house. We felt if we found some land somewhere we were both comfortable with and found it at a reasonable price, it would not only be less expensive, but the move outside London would also come with a better quality of life. After all we had been through, we just wanted a quiet life in surroundings that were serene for us. That old cliché, life is too short, had a different meaning for us after all we had been through. I cannot count the number of times I would settle in bed and say, "Thank you Lord for not making me a widow." I'd said this so many times over the years. At the end of the year at our December 31st night service at church, I would often sing in praise, but would nearly always say how grateful I was that I hadn't been left a widow as I was giving my testimony of gratitude for the year.

I became quite ill with a bad flu virus for about two months, shortly after Eddie had his operation. I then contracted bronchitis that was treated with three different inhalers as my shortness of breath wasn't improving. To top it off, I had sciatica in my back and left leg and had to use crutches while Eddie was still in hospital. I still insisted on going to see him even when he asked me to rest and the hospital staff reassured me they were taking good enough care of him.

Chapter 6. Home Sweet Home

While Eddie was in hospital, a three-part drama was shown on Sky about a woman whose husband was murdered shortly after they were married. The wife had to find out who killed her husband after it came to light that he was living a double life working for a firm with less-than-favourable business dealings. It was a brilliant drama, so much so I told Eddie he had to watch it. He had all these fancy things on his phone to be able to set his phone to record his programmes to watch from hospital. It made no sense to me because I hardly watched TV, so never learnt to do all that. I only found out about the drama because the telly happened to have been left on and the storyline just caught my attention. I was drawn to the strength of this woman. I was astounded at how determined she was. I just couldn't imagine, I told myself, that I would have an ounce of this woman's strength to be able to fight so hard for the truth. I knew what it felt like to love your husband so how was it possible to be in such grief but be so, well...strong? It intrigued me, but of course I didn't need to dwell on that so much, because that wasn't my story, was it?

Eddie spent a total of two months in hospital and was discharged a few days before Christmas. Though the operation was successful, he wasn't making progress as quickly as they had liked so, after the operation, he was transferred to a rehabilitation centre to get him used to the hip replacement. Surprisingly, the hip replacement was fine, but there was still a lot of pain that couldn't be explained. After seeing a neurologist and an orthopaedic consultant, further tests were carried out and it was finally narrowed down to a muscle that had also been causing the pain. A minor procedure was to be carried out on the 17 January 2019 to finally resolve the debilitating pain Eddie had been forced to live with. The procedure was carried out and everything went well. He came home to recover, and all was well in the Sillah household.

***

I had an event I was running on the Saturday 19 January in Kensington. It was a one-day workshop I'd put together the year before called *Rewriting History*. I would typically have about 25-30 delegates where I would use my skills as a transformational life coach to assist them in identifying and then process mapping common trends in behaviour that would result in decisions and actions being taken that didn't serve them. I created this workshop because of my own experience in repeating certain behaviours that left me feeling as if I had underachieved or hadn't reached my full potential by the end of the year. I was sick and tired of entering a new year with so much expectation but then nothing to really show for it by the end of the year. *Rewriting History*, for me, was the ability to change my narrative on certain aspects of my life.

I had put off writing my first book for so long for so many different reasons, but it was when I literally had a mind and attitude shift that I was able to write that book without procrastinating. My mission was to focus on at least one big win so that, come the end of the year, no matter what would have happened, I would have something to be proud of that was symbolic of progress.

The workshop went extremely well. The feedback was excellent and everyone who attended was so enthusiastic and optimistic about their futures. It was such a blessing to be a

Chapter 6. Home Sweet Home

part of that. I was extremely tired at the end of it all though and just wanted to get back home and get some rest. I had been checking on Eddie throughout the day and he was doing fine.

When I got home, we caught up with me giving him a complete account of what the day had been like and showing him a video of the private VIP breakfast we'd had. He was happy it had all gone so well and was a little annoyed I didn't put my paperwork away and relax. I was tired, that I couldn't deny. My whole body ached, and I felt like I was now running on empty. It had been a very intense workshop, with people sharing so much of themselves that the atmosphere created was really special with great energy. Being at home was where I needed to be or, really being in bed is where I needed to be, so I retired early.

I woke up on Sunday 20 January to a very tired and irritable husband. The neighbours were once again playing their music loudly and it had kept Eddie up for most of the night. Unfortunately, the living room where Eddie slept shared a wall with their living room and they just weren't civilised enough to understand that a person who was unwell needed rest. I had knocked on their door countless times to tell them to keep the noise down, but they just didn't seem to get it. I told Eddie I would go 'round there but he always dissuaded me so I would sneak out when he wasn't aware. At 10 o'clock in the morning, the music was still at full blast, not what anyone needed to hear first thing on a Sunday, especially after the exhausting day I had had the day before.

I pulled on a pair of jeans under my dressing gown and slipped my feet into some slippers. As soon as I was about to open the door, the doorbell rang. There was a young man in front of me saying he was from next door and wanting to let me know they were going to have a party…meaning there might be some noise.

"You should thank the Lord Jesus you came 'round here 'cos I was just about to knock on your door. If you're going to have a party and be playing music so early, you really should give people notice so they can make alternative arrangements and go out to avoid the noise. My husband isn't well, and your music has kept him up half the night."

They hadn't turned the music down before coming to my house, so I invited the young man in to hear how loud it sounded in the hallway. Even he had to admit it was bad. The wall clock vibrated, so you can imagine how difficult it was to relax and function in the house with such a racket. He apologised for the inconvenience and said the party was for his little sister and that it wouldn't be a late one.

"I'm not an unreasonable or horrible neighbour. I would never have a problem with a child's party but just give me advance notice so I know how to organise myself."

We exchanged pleasantries before he left and I went up to Eddie. A couple of hours later, a very good friend of mine who I consider to be more of a sister, paid us a visit. I had been on at her that she hadn't cooked her special soup for me so she should try to bring some 'round that afternoon if she could. I heard the doorbell and answered it; there she was with the biggest pot of soup full of all the things I loved in it. I stayed in the kitchen while she went upstairs to supposedly just say hello to Eddie. I knew how that was going to end; Eddie loved anyone that loved me so he was particularly close to all my friends. After about an hour, she came downstairs to tell me

Chapter 6. Home Sweet Home

she was off. I hurled some playful insults at her and joked how Eddie always stole all my friends. After placing the soup in containers to pack in the freezer, Eddie sent me off to rest as he could see I was still exhausted. He was going to give up on sleeping and watch the football instead.

I rested a little then fixed him a late lunch before going back for more rest. Before retiring to bed for the night, I always checked if Eddie wanted anything. It just made things easier for him if I gave him whatever he needed to save him the trouble. He couldn't manage the kettle and hot water and coordinating himself to negotiate the stairs, so I always did that for him. However, I was about to doze off when my phone rang, just after 11 o'clock. It was a dear friend of mine calling from the States.

"Oh hi! I'll call you back in a mo. I'm just gonna check if Eddie needs anything."

I knew I was going to be back on that call in a few minutes because Eddie had hardly rested in two days so I knew he would be tired. I went downstairs and popped my head behind the door. "You're not sleeping?" I was shocked and surprised because he was sat bolt upright on the sofa, arms folded across his chest, wide awake and laughing at something on telly; not a sight I was expecting to see.

"You don't look like someone who's ready to sleep," I said. So, I sat next to him.

Before I knew it, at some point he had his feet on my lap and we talked and talked…and talked. We spoke for the best part of two-and-a-half hours – about my plans for the year ahead, him and other stuff; stuff that would both become a source of comfort and a source of great pain, because it was the last conversation I was to have with my husband. What we spoke about was so special that I've only shared it with my children and very close family. I believe God knew Eddie was being called home, so He gave me something for my children and I to hold onto – a bittersweet memory that one day will be a source of peace for all of us.

I bade Eddie goodnight at 1:30 in the morning, declaring with fake sternness, "You? I'm not going to follow you! If I follow you, I'll be here until I hear the birds singing and I have a project to complete. I'm going to bed!"

Chapter 7

Darkness

Monday 21 January 2019.

I woke up at 9:08 in the morning. I know that because I have a habit of reaching for my mobile phone and checking the time before I do anything. It doesn't matter if I don't intend to wake up, I'll always check my phone. Then I thought I heard Eddie call for me but wasn't sure. The next call was loud and clear, and I rushed downstairs. I asked him what was wrong, and he said he just wasn't feeling too well. He took my hand and used it to wipe his forehead.

"See how I'm sweating! Pray for me," he said, and I did. "Put your hand on my forehead and pray for me."

So, I prayed for him again. Then he asked me to lay down beside him and I squeezed myself beside him and lay there for a couple of minutes at most. He really didn't look well, so I called the ambulance. While I was talking to the operator, Eddie had a funny turn. I had never seen that happen to him before. I thought I'd lost him for a moment, but he came 'round after a couple of minutes. For the first time I was really scared. I was panicking in fact as I ran down the stairs to open the front door. It was just the two of us at home so there would be no one else to open it when the paramedics arrived, and I didn't want to leave Eddie alone. I kept talking to him and telling him he was going to be okay and that I had called an ambulance. I rang them back because by now at least ten minutes had passed. The lady on the other end of the phone was trying to reassure me, but it wasn't working. I was trying to keep calm, but couldn't; I was just so, so frightened.

After what seemed like an eternity, what I thought was the ambulance, but was really the first responders, arrived to help my husband. A young girl, no more than five feet tall and slightly built, came to attend to Eddie. She did all the necessary checks and said it was serious and that we needed to get him to the hospital as soon as possible. She asked me if there was anyone that could come and wait with me and give me some support. This rage and indignation rose up through my body when she said that.

"Why? Why would I need anyone to offer me support? I've looked after my husband by myself for nearly four years. I don't need anyone to support me!"

But somehow, in my heart, I knew there was something wrong based on the way she asked me that question. Eddie had passed out a couple of times by now but had come around and was responsive when asked if he knew what was going on.

"Yes, yes, I can hear you. I know you're trying to move me," and that was true, he knew what was happening.

Shortly after, two sets of feet came racing up the stairs, into the living room and Eddie was then taken to the ambulance. My understanding was that it was urgent, and Eddie needed to be rushed to hospital, but I was asked to wait in the house.

Chapter 7. Darkness

I didn't understand. I didn't wait in the house. I paced in front of and around the ambulance. My neighbour on the right side of my house came outside to ask what was happening. I was barely able to string a sentence together, but she got the gist of what I was trying to tell her.

By now 25 minutes or so had passed. The ambulance crew were all in the ambulance and I couldn't understand why there was no rush, why there were no sirens blazing and cars being overtaken to get my husband to hospital. I remember letting out an almighty scream. My neighbour came rushing out again, refusing to leave me out in the biting January cold. I reluctantly went inside her house and refused to touch any water or tea that she tried so desperately to get me to drink. My brain was still trying to process why I wasn't allowed to be with my husband and why the sirens weren't going off. I saw another car pull up next to the ambulance – that took the total to three cars parked by our home for Eddie.

Eventually the young paramedic came back and said Eddie's heart had stopped and that they were doing all they could to revive him. I fainted. When I came to, I heard the young lady hurriedly ask my neighbour if she would be okay to look after me as they had to leave immediately. I was able to get into my neighbour's car with her daughter, who happened to be a newly-qualified doctor. We ended up directly behind the ambulance and I could see them performing CPR. Something suddenly dawned on me and I turned to speak to my neighbour's daughter.

"It's been too long," I whispered. "Even if they revive him now, he'll be brain dead."

She didn't look into my eyes but gave a slight nod of her head.

I picked up my phone and rang the one other person Eddie loved so dearly – his sister. I told her Eddie was really unwell and it wasn't looking good. I heard her scream a scream that sounded all too familiar, because that same sound had escaped my own lips shortly before. I heard the phone crash and someone else come on the line. I repeated what I had said to the stranger on the other end of the line while my sister-in-law cried and screamed hysterically in the background; it was the hardest call I've ever had to make.

After about ten minutes, the ambulance took off with the crew still working on Eddie because I could still see the silhouette of one bobbing up and down. We drove to North Middlesex Hospital still behind the ambulance…there were still no sirens. When we finally arrived, we reported to the receptionist who seemed to be expecting us. We were directed to a room and asked to wait. About 20 minutes after our arrival, a young Asian doctor asked me to confirm my name. I did. I was asked to sit down…and he said the words I didn't want to hear.

"I'm sorry Mrs Sillah. We did all we could for your husband but…, "

To be honest, I can't remember beyond those words. All I remember, very vividly, are the tiny spots before my eyes and darkness enveloping the room. Everything was spinning and I couldn't make it stop. I felt my jaw tighten. I thanked him curtly and got up to go to the private room reserved for the bereaved, where I was to wait for Eddie to be brought back to me in the adjoining room.

Chapter 7. Darkness

***

"Mrs Sillah, if you're ready you can come through."

I wanted to be left alone. I stood there looking at the man I'd spent 17 years of my life with and now lying lifeless before me, but with the most peaceful smile on his lips. I laid my head on his chest and kissed them. I ran my hands over his head and held his hand. I wanted to remember everything about him while he was still warm. I couldn't believe he had left me. After all the suffering and hard work, after all the battles I had fought for so long to nurse him back to health, he just left me…and I couldn't understand why.

Then I remembered – I had to call my daughter. I'd already called my son who was on his way to the hospital, as well as some members of my family and a cousin of Eddie's. My pastors and two of my close friends were called, one of them being the friend who had been laughing and joking with Eddie less than 24 hours before.

The shock and devastation was palpable in that room. I can't remember if I called my daughter's school or if someone else had done that for me but I remember asking for her to be brought to the hospital. I wanted to preserve the world she had known all her life, for it to remain still for just a little while longer but I couldn't hold off for too long. She was brought to me and I told her that her daddy had gone. It was the most heart-wrenching thing ever. Even as I write, I can feel the nausea rising; I felt complete and utter devastation for my husband's only daughter.

My son sat silently in the bereavement room which by now was getting a tad overcrowded. He eventually got up and said he wanted to spend time with his dad, alone. He was there for a while. I still looked around that room like I was a visitor at someone else's grief gathering, but it was mine. It was actually mine. When my son came out of the room, I sat with Eddie. I wept in utter disbelief now, refusing to leave his side. He looked so peaceful. I knew how much he leaned on me and I didn't want him to feel alone, so I waited until they came to take him away. When the porters came and covered him up, my legs buckled for the second time that day. I had to let him go alone – this time I couldn't go with him. It just wasn't real.

We all solemnly filed out of the bereavement room in a daze. I couldn't bring myself to speak to anyone so Eddie's cousin took the calls that came through on my phone. One of the calls was from the brother whose daughter Eddie and I had taken on holiday with us in Portugal when he fell ill. He had offered to come to the house but I was too drained and more concerned about my children to have anyone come to my home at a time like that. I asked Eddie's cousin to tell hi, that I was in no fit state to see anyone. We proceeded to our respective cars and began the journey back home.

★★★

I walked through the doors of the living room and there was no Eddie sitting there. The house was cold but this time the cold felt different, as if it could enter the very core of my being. I managed to clear up the mess in the living room and then climb the stairs to my room. I sat on the bed and stared into space. I knew the news of Eddie's death would spread like wildfire because he was a very well-loved and liked human being, a super-popular character. I also knew that because of

Chapter 7. Darkness

my work, the news would hit home for many people on my side too. As I wasn't ready for an influx of people asking me what had happened, I put a statement out on my personal Facebook page.

My life has changed forever today. The love of my life, my husband, the one I cared for, fought with, teased, laughed with, loved with my whole heart – he asked me to pray for him and within minutes, he was gone. My husband left me today ever so suddenly and without any warning to go and rest with the angels. I would like to be left alone to make sense of how I became a widow and single parent at 47 on the 21st of January 2019. Eddie…I was dedicated and committed to you. I fought for you in every way, but this time I lost. I'm sorry I failed you in this fight. Sleep well. Know I love you so much…until we meet again…

Sleep came out of pure exhaustion. At some point I woke up and for a few moments, everything was normal. Then it hit me – *Dilys, you lost your husband yesterday.* I sat bolt upright on my bed and tried to process what I had just told myself. Then, I wept like I've never wept before. The pain I felt in the very core and depths of my soul cannot be described in words. There are no words to describe what it felt like to have your heart ripped out and cut in two and then one half shoved back into your chest demanding that you function as if you have your whole heart pumping away. I was confused. I was in shock. I was in the belly of despair. I was in the pit of devastation. I couldn't breathe. I remember that feeling so vividly; the feeling of suffocation, but just about being able to draw enough breath not to pass out.

My phone went off and I saw I had a message from my husband's brother who had called the day before.

8:06.

I read the first few lines of the message as the notification bar popped up on my screen, demanding to know what arrangements were being made for my husband. I could feel the blood rising and the grief being replaced with an intense anger. I was so angry. I was so mad. How dare he? My husband had been gone for less than 24 hours. How the hell would I have made any bloody arrangements for him? I could barely get my head around the fact that he really had left me. Little did I know that this was the beginning of the worst kind of treatment I would ever be subjected or witness to.

I quickly called my husband's cousin and yelled down the phone that I had just received a message from Eddie's brother demanding to be informed of the arrangements for his burial. I couldn't fathom the insensitivity and cruelty of it all and asked him to call Eddie's brother and warn him not to ring my phone or message me. I couldn't speak and I certainly wasn't able to discuss funeral arrangements for a man I couldn't even accept was dead. My husband's cousin did a good job reassuring me and I eventually calmed down. I went on to point out that this was the same brother who hadn't visited Eddie the whole time he was ill, and therefore I felt it was an absolute cheek and gross disrespect to take the position of concerned brother now that he was gone. It was at this point that I mentioned that by rights, if he had an iota of decency, he would be apologising for his lack of support and regard for my husband before demanding anything. The cousin and I said our goodbyes and I reiterated that he should please let

Chapter 7. Darkness

the family know that he was the point of contact for them; I really wasn't in any position to speak to anyone. My son had come home with me the night before, so he came up to my room to find out what was going on. He was and still is an amazing source of strength for both his sister and me. He did all he could do to try to calm me down.

It wasn't long before an influx of mourners started coming to the house. I just couldn't get my head round why they were there and then I realised why. It sounds ridiculous that my brain would be working in that way, but that was honestly how I felt. The more people that came to offer their condolences, the more I couldn't understand why they were there.

★★★

In the Ghanaian tradition, we have mourners officially come to the house on the seventh day. It was so hard for me to have that conversation with my family to discuss what we needed to do to get the house arranged to receive guests. Eddie was hugely popular, and I know many people through social media and the advocacy and activism work I do. So, there was going to be a lot of visitors but I never thought that there would be as many as had actually walked through my doors. Someone suggested we may need to hire a hall for the seven-day ceremony, but I resented what I was having to do and the attention that came with it, so I refused. What I did agree to was having guests come to the house over the weekend instead. We hired a few chairs and put them around the living room so at least some of the seating could be taken care of.

One of the hardest things I had to do, that still brings a lump to my throat, happened on the Saturday morning. A long black traditional kaftan was made for me to wear; I'll never forget my sister taking the outfit out of the plastic covering and laying it on the bed. I stood there looking at it and not believing I had to wear it for Eddie, my Eddie. I looked at it in a daze and felt hot tears just streaming down my face; I think this was probably the moment that stark reality hit. It was at this moment the realisation that I was officially a widow, stared me in the face. Having something as physical and as tangible as a black dress made it undeniable, inescapable, that I was indeed…a widow. I slipped the dress over my head and picked up the black scarf that was laid beside the dress on the bed and tied it over my head. By this time there were guests waiting for me. I took a deep, deep breath and proceeded to go down the stairs into the living room.

There were all these faces, all these people crying, in shock, overwhelmed to be in my home to pay respects to my husband. I cannot tell you how much of an out-of-body experience that felt like. I didn't have the strength to put on a brave face or do the other clichéd things you're told to do like 'be strong.' Oh, how I hated all those phrases. I didn't want to be strong. I wanted to curl up and die. I wanted to scream at the very top of my lungs until I had run out of breath with no sound coming out – that's what I wanted to do. Strong? For who and for what? If ever there was a time I felt weak, abandoned, alone and deserted, it was then. I remember one strange emotion and that was the feeling of nakedness; I felt so exposed. I literally felt like I was standing naked in that room. I'd been with Eddie for 17 years and even though he wasn't well for the last few years of that time, his presence in my life as a husband and as a man, as my covering – was never

Chapter 7. Darkness

in dispute. Now that he was gone, I felt there was no shield or protection and I was exposed for all to see my nakedness. It was an exposure that said, 'Now you can get her. She has nobody. She is nobody. She is yours now.'

The guests could only see me as the broken woman I was and, by God, was I broken; in fact, I was shattered – emotionally, mentally, spiritually and physically. In a matter of days, I had dropped about half a stone. My face was gaunt and my eyes hollow. I couldn't face food at all. The thought of food just made my stomach tighten. Everyone begged me to eat for strength but I didn't want to be strong, so it was okay that I didn't eat. I didn't need strength. I needed my husband and food didn't have the power to bring him back, so what was the point of eating?

I took my seat in the very place my husband had occupied just days before and let the formalities begin. In the Ashanti tradition, where my father is from, there are certain protocols that are followed upon the death of a family member. Mourners will typically come to the house to find out if what they have heard about the death of a loved one or family member was indeed true. They do not take the word of a third party as gospel; they must go to the family of the person who is alleged to have passed away to confirm what they have been told. What this means is that someone is appointed to speak on behalf of the family. The person who has been bereaved, in this case me, the widow, doesn't answer any questions. I am also not permitted to shake the hands of any mourners; when they enter the gathering, they must shake hands of all those seated from the right side of the room, working their way round but skipping me and going to the next person.

The mourners would bring with them a monetary donation or drinks such as water, other soft drinks or alcohol. This was done to minimise the financial burden on the mourning family. It was gruelling because each time the doorbell rang and the person came up those stairs, they would be asked the reason for their visit and what they were doing at the time the news reached them. Their response would always be the same.

"We were at home and we heard something that caused us great concern so we said we would come and enquire as to what if we heard is really true."

The appointed spokesperson would respond each time. "Thank you for coming here today. Yes, unfortunately all that you've heard is true…,"

Then the details of my husband's passing would be duly recounted, over and over and over again for as many times as was required by however many people would come to my home to pay their respects.

What I found so bitter and difficult was hearing that my life had seemingly ended, as well as that of my husband. This was repeated like an open wound being picked at over and over and there not being a damn thing I could do about it. It was hard, it was so damn hard. I couldn't lie about how bad it was.

Chapter 8

The Loud Silent War

A couple of days had passed when it started. You hear so many stories of families going to war when a loved one passes away but Eddie's loss was so devastating, I naively thought that the only emotions anyone could have was profound sadness and a deep feeling of loss. Like I said, I was naïve and stupid.

The first call I got was from an aunt of Eddie's – a lovely lady he was particularly close to. When I had my daughter, she was one of two aunts that visited. She cooked pot-loads of food I could eat without too much hassle because I was breastfeeding. I grew to love her myself because it was evident why Eddie was so close to her. She was very gentle and softly-spoken and was always so welcoming and polite to me whenever we visited her. Because Eddie worked with elderly people in his old job and helped with financial assessments, he helped his aunt a lot; widowed herself, she would rely on Eddie to do the 'manly' things around the house and give her whatever support she needed. She was one person who called to ask how Eddie was doing often. If she wasn't so ill, she probably would have come to visit a lot more. The news of her nephew's passing hit her really hard. My heart broke for her because I knew how much she loved and more so how much she would miss him. So, I was particularly upset when I heard her on the other end of the phone so upset she could hardly speak.

My aunty proceeded to tell me that some of the family members had held a meeting about me, saying I was intentionally making myself unavailable and that she was supporting me in disrespecting the family. It was heartbreaking to hear her protests over the phone trying to convince me, between sobs, of her innocence. I obviously knew this was a load of rubbish but to be honest, was too exhausted to give what they were saying any serious thought. I did my best to calm her down and tell her to ignore these people.

I wasn't really answering my phone. By this time, I always had someone with me to ensure I ate, even though that was futile, and that I would rest between visitors to the house. I explained this to Aunty and said if anyone really needed to speak to me, there was Eddie's cousin. I think it was around this time I found out Eddie's brother had gone to the family to say I didn't want to speak to them, and Aunty had somehow been dragged into a forming feud I had no idea even existed. In my naivety, I dismissed it as being something that was just trying to zap her energy and not to give it any thought; little did I know a war was being waged and I was the enemy.

I noticed some of the phone calls I did receive all seemed to refer to the fact that I was hard to get through to. I thought it was such a grossly stupid and entitled statement to make under the circumstances. I had just lost my husband! Who in

Chapter 8. The Loud Silent War

their right mind would expect me to be answering the phone as if I now lived for the moment the phone would ring for me to receive condolences? How ridiculously stupid!

I wasn't really able to engage in much conversation so I did a lot of listening. Well, I say a lot, but I could probably only manage about a minute, by which time I would pass the phone to whoever was sitting beside me or was looking after me at that time. More reports of my 'behaviour' were coming to my attention and that's when I started to pay attention. Early one morning, I received the following text message from a cousin of Eddie's:

Good morning Dilys. My deepest sympathy. May the Lord give you strength during this difficult time. The reason I am texting you is about the chaos you have created for Edward's funeral. This should have been a time for us to come together and mourn Edward. The family is ready to stand by you and your daughter. Believe me or not you are still in shock as none of us would have ever imagined Edward, a young and vibrant man would die at such a tender age. Do not listen to people who would leave you all by yourself soon after you buried Edward.

Finally, I would like to know if Edward left Lasting Power of Attorney to you over his funeral plans; specifically for ***** and family members not to attend his funeral. If he did, can you please send me the certificate number so I can go and check at the court of protection. Otherwise you have no right to stop anyone from attending Edward's funeral. The family still love and respect you as Edward's wife and mother of her beloved daughter. I am looking forward to hearing from you by the end of today.

I was in the living room when this message came through on Eddie's phone; two amazing 'sister friends', as I like to call them, were with me when I got the text. I showed them.

"What kind of stupid nonsense is this? Can you imagine what this idiot has just sent me? Who the bloody hell does she think she is? Who the bloody hell does this stupid bitch think she is?!"

There was a split second's silence and my concerned friends asked me what was wrong. I was so angry, I couldn't speak. I passed the phone to them to read the message and their jaws dropped. They couldn't understand how or why anyone would feel it appropriate to send such a disgustingly insensitive and disrespectful message to a woman who had just lost her husband, and quite frankly, neither could I. I had only met this individual once, twice at best and why or how she felt so entitled to send me such a message, I knew not. Who had appointed her as a spokesperson? She clearly felt she had more hairs on her chest than the rest of whoever she was representing. Well, she was about to get them plucked like a Christmas turkey.

My hands were shaking when I dialled her number; I was ready to let rip but the number went to voicemail. I don't recall if I left a message but I do remember sending a polite text to tell her I was getting in touch as I had received her message.

I got a response back saying she was in a meeting and would call back around lunchtime or so. I waited a while and called back and luckily for me but unluckily for her, she answered the phone. After she got the pleasantries out of the way of expressing her condolences and mentioning the aunty who had given her the blessing in sending the message

Chapter 8. The Loud Silent War

to me, I asked what exactly she meant by the text. I could sense the embarrassment in her voice and was proven right by her inability to actually repeat its contents once asked to do so. She cowardly advised that she didn't want to repeat it but wanted to be involved in the planning of the funeral. I respectfully kept quiet while she went on to tell me how my life would never be the same after losing Eddie.

"You will never be the same. Your life will never be the same; you are not going to be the same."

I got it. She didn't think I would ever be the same!

I continued to listen intently and asked permission to speak once her theatrics were over with. She began to interrupt me once I started to lay out my defence as to why her message to me was inappropriate, insensitive and a downright insult. After gaining some order, as she was constantly trying to speak over me, I explained my reasons for not allowing Eddie's brother to attend the funeral by giving her the facts of how he treated Eddie after he fell ill on holiday with his daughter; it was Eddie's brother she had referred to in her message to me. There is nothing like speaking someone's language when you really want to communicate with them so I switched from English to Krio – the lingo spoken in most parts of Sierra Leone. I don't know if it was just what I was saying that shocked her, or the fact that I was saying it in her language as a Ghanaian woman, because the wind left her sails pretty quickly. There was complete and utter silence during the last half of that conversation on her part. I had been eerily calm when I'd first started speaking, having listened to her contrived defence of also not being able to 'get hold' of me. She and the rest of them all sounded like a stuck record and for me, they desperately needed to start singing a different tune.

It turned out that prior to the phone call there had been several meetings with certain members of Eddie's family. I didn't know half of them so couldn't understand why they felt they knew me well enough to decide I was an enemy or didn't want them to participate in the funeral. Eddie's brother was the initiator of the confusion by relaying a message I had never given, giving bullets to those with guns. My position was very simple: I felt the treatment of my husband by his so called brother was wrong, shameful and callous just as I had made clear in the conversation I had with his cousin. I refused to be disrespected by anyone, and that meant *anyone*!

I hadn't been disrespectful to any members of my husband's family therefore I wasn't about to take what I hadn't dished out. As far as I was concerned, for my husband's memory to be afforded the level of respect I believe he was entitled to, his brother should apologise for his behaviour since learning of my husband's passing. He had declined to apologise, even after some of my other in-laws had tried to reason with him and point out how bad his actions really looked. I had also pointed out that his apology would go some way in showing he was remorseful for the disgraceful, despicable and deplorable way he had treated Eddie during his illness. I understand he said to Eddie's favourite aunt: "Over my dead body will I ever apologise." That was good to know because there was either going to be another funeral if he hadn't rendered that apology or the security firm I was planning on hiring would have their hands full.

Chapter 8. The Loud Silent War

I felt better after letting the cheeky mare have it. I was like a raging bull for days. It's in retrospect that I realise that if there ever was a period when I'd gone through the anger phase of grief, that would have been it. The whole debacle gave me the space to channel that strong emotion the way I needed to. Of course, in between there was even more happening; they upped the ante in a bid to make me crumble, going for the lowest blow to see if I could stand under the weight of hatred and misguided anger that they directed towards me.

What I found really offensive was the fact that I'd cared for Eddie single-handedly. Not once did I ask for help, whether financial or physical or even for the odd prayer! I asked for nothing and I demanded and expected nothing. We were both private and proud people so we dealt with our issues and challenges with dignity. I could not fathom how some idiot could send me such an inflammatory message, when by their own admission, they had only met me a couple of times in the years I was with Eddie. On top of that, they claimed to have been close to my husband? Not once did this individual ever pay her beloved cousin a visit or send a message to ask if there was anything we needed or anything they could do for us. Yet, as soon as the person died, they suddenly became a voice for him? I don't think so!

Eddie had another aunt who was allegedly the brains behind this witch-hunt (and I use the word "brains" loosely) with the cousin and other family members. I had never cared for her much, having met her a couple of times. When Eddie and I were getting married, we hired a minibus for her and some other relatives, but she didn't turn up. I found it incredibly crass and disrespectful, as did Eddie. They never declined the wedding invitation but thought it okay to not show up, with no word of warning or explanation. On the day of the wedding there was one table that was empty as a result. I think for Eddie and for me, to be honest, the parameters under which certain relationships fell and how they would be conducted became clear that day. Eddie had always been very, very hurt by that but in all honesty, he was glad to have caught onto them. So, it was not surprising that this woman was so hell-bent on causing the most hurt and confusion. She never once called to offer her condolences. She never once enquired about our welfare. She never once called Eddie during his three-and-a-half-years of ill health to ask how he was progressing, if he was progressing at all.

What she did do was appoint herself as the 'chief mourner' on behalf of the family.

Let me explain. The position of chief mourner in these circumstances would be me, his wife. It would not be his mother or sister and most certainly not a random aunty who had made herself as scarce as a seat on the Central Line during rush-hour. What I found most sad and offensive was learning that she was accepting monetary donations when she received guests at a home that was not even her own. What made it even worse was the fact that my elderly mother-in-law in Sierra Leone never received a dime of that money – money which I consider blood money and received under the most despicable and deceitful of circumstances.

What many people didn't know was that Eddie's younger brother in Sierra Leone also died suddenly, seven weeks later, after a short illness. We were once again faced with unexpected grief and death. I had never met this brother as I had never

Chapter 8. The Loud Silent War

been to Sierra Leone and Eddie hadn't gone back there since he was 21 years old. I thought that this aunt would have been moved with enough compassion to at least send some money to an elderly woman faced with burying her only two sons. But no, that never happened. What instead happened was her best friend sending two strangers to my mother-in-law the day she was burying her second son to slander my name. I love that old lady's spirit though because she had only one thing to say to them, which was and I paraphrase, "Dilys I know. You I don't." She didn't give them audience and they left. Shockingly insensitive and downright wicked but I was becoming all too familiar with how certain relatives behaved.

It wasn't enough that all this was going on while I was trying to quietly grieve for my husband. I started getting really vile messages on Facebook and Instagram. I mean really disgusting messages, telling me they were glad my husband was dead and that my children were left fatherless. The bastards writing this filth even went as far as calling my daughter a bitch and even made references to rape in their messages. Now there is one thing I can't stand as much as liars, and that's bullies. I despise them with the very core of my being. It doesn't matter if I'm not the victim; I will never stand by and let it happen under my watch. I started a whole charity because of the online bullying of a rape victim so that should tell you the kind of person I am when it comes to that sort of thing. Unfortunately, the animals that started trolling me on social media didn't know that about me. They thought they would get me at my most vulnerable and pile on the pressure so badly that I would crumple and fall. They had no idea who I really was.

Initially I would delete the messages as soon as they popped up. Then they got a bit more frequent and almost desperate. It was at this point I also decided to change tactics. I thought I would give these animals a taste of their own medicine. I always felt I knew who was behind the messages and didn't believe it was one person, so I started to taunt them just as much as they thought they could taunt me. They would set up fake accounts and bombard me with messages. Some of the content must have been too abusive because on occasion, the messages would be removed before I would have a chance to read them. I didn't tell many people what was going on because I didn't want them to worry. Was I bothered by the messages? Truthfully? Not really. I just felt those behind it were so incredibly evil and demonic, with more than a few nuts and bolts loose that I couldn't imagine giving such beasts my power.

I was mad as hell when my son came to me with a message the bullies had sent him. That's when things changed. I thought of how my daughter would feel if she was on social media and these things were thrown at her. She was only a little girl and there's no way she would have had the level of resilience to deal with that kind of cyber-bullying, or any other kind of bullying to be perfectly honest. Thankfully, my son inherited my acid tongue so he dealt with them and they never messaged him again. Clearly though, I was so special that the messages kept coming through to me.

I was told to 'ignore' them because I was grieving. Why should I ignore them? These people were bullies. Why do we tell children to stand up to bullies but when adults decide to exhibit the same behaviour, we are basically told to allow

Chapter 8. The Loud Silent War

them to get away with murder? It made no sense to me to do that. Why live in a state of anxiety, constantly looking over my shoulder, not knowing when the next message was going to pop up? There was something that drove me to fight my corner that meant more to me than anything – Eddie did not know his wife to be a coward.

Eddie's family in London, the ones I hardly knew, weren't satisfied with the fact that I didn't seem to be crumbling, so, they decided, for whatever reason, to 'report' me to one of the family elders back in Sierra Leone. They had reported that Eddie was unhappy in the marriage and had wanted to leave. They weren't expecting to be asked by a man who had never met me, which one of them my husband had confided in? They all dispersed one by one when none of them could come up with a shred of evidence to substantiate the ridiculous notion Eddie was about to leave me. To go where exactly, I don't know. Anything that could be said to either tarnish my reputation or call into question the state of my marriage was the new low they had sunk to.

They didn't leave it there; having had no luck with the first family elder, they decided to go to the Alhaji. Eddie's parents were Muslim though he was raised as a Christian. The Alhaji essentially is the highest authority in their family. They faced yet another brick wall with him and were threatened to be cursed if they didn't stop harassing me; in their culture that was a big deal.

What is also worth mentioning here, and where the Sierra Leonean tradition differs from the Ghanaian tradition, is that the body of the deceased belongs to the spouse, not the family – in Ghana the body belongs to the family and not the spouse. So, Sierra Leonean tradition follows British law, where the widow or widower typically has all rights over the proceedings and burial of their husband or wife. Eddie's family members who had waged war against me didn't know I was aware of this 'minor' detail, which essentially meant they had no real say over burial rights and proceedings. In fact, they were supposed to have observed certain parts of their own tradition, which they had miserably failed to do.

There was no cooking of food by my in-laws when Eddie first passed away, neither were there any bags of rice and other provisions that are typically brought with the mourners to the home of the person who has died. My argument when those members of the family were trying to exert their authority over me was that they had failed in upholding their own tradition which meant I could ignore other aspects of tradition too. Furthermore, their failure to respect some of these traditions showed contempt for the person who had died and the family he had left behind.

I had a choice to make. I could do the 'done thing' which was remaining quiet and letting others speak on my behalf, pretending they could fight my battles better than I could, or I could stand up for myself. As I said, Eddie knew I was a warrior who could always hold my own. I felt like I would have been letting him down immensely by allowing myself to morph into a doormat. Eddie had to be proud of me. I had fought for him all this time and now I just had a little way to go. I knew I could do it. I knew I had it within me and had enough resilience to withstand the fiery darts of the enemy. I knew I had what it took to do right by my husband and his memory.

Chapter 9

Over the Rainbow

So much of my attention was being diverted from my children because of what was being done to me that I didn't realise how much it was affecting them. I also didn't realise how much of my peace was being stolen and how much I was being taken away from planning my husband's funeral. I just wanted peace and quiet in my head so I could deal with the huge task I had ahead of me in making all the arrangements to lay him to rest.

I wasn't really in any fit state to plan the funeral on my own, that was obvious. It was killing me to even think that was the task I had ahead. It got harder for me to deal with the situation because I felt time was pulling me away from Eddie. Every day the sun rose and set was another day that time pulled and separated the two of us. Time that was to be this great healer was my number one enemy. It was harder and harder for me to say, "Yesterday Eddie was here" or "Last week Eddie and I did...." Time meant I was having to rely on memories that were fast becoming clouded and jumbled because of the trauma of his very sudden and painful death.

I remember not wanting to even leave the house because I felt ashamed and exposed. I went through some pretty illogically-logical emotions in the beginning and because I felt them, I had to honour them. They were too powerful and confident in their existence in my head to be denied.

★★★

A funeral director came to the house and spoke to me about what type of service I wanted. I was thankful that he was an extremely lovely man who, incidentally, had lost his wife suddenly too. He talked me through everything I needed to know and made an impossible situation slightly bearable. There was one problem though – I had to physically go to the funeral home to sign the paperwork and go through other bits and pieces such as the type of design I would like for the order of service. This part of the transaction could not be conducted in my living room. The wall of isolation I was slowly building around myself was getting higher and higher and it was probably my saving grace that I was forced to leave the house at the point. If that opportunity had not arrived then, I was well on my way to developing a real fear of going outside.

As I said, I had some amazing people around me, and in particular, two ladies decided it would be a good idea to form a committee to plan the funeral. A WhatsApp group was quickly put together and roles and tasks were designated to ensure Eddie's send-off would be what he would have wanted. I would also be relieved of some of the energy required to bury a loved one because I didn't have that strength to do it alone. I immediately felt the burden of planning the intricate

Chapter 9. Over the Rainbow

parts of the funeral slowly lifting. My job was just to nod and shake my head to relay what I wanted or didn't want.

I had to decide where I wanted my husband buried, what type of grave I wanted to lay him in...whether it was going to be an earth grave or a lawn grave...I didn't care! I didn't want to give permission to anyone to put my husband in the ground. It was unfathomable to me how I was expected to think like that but that was something only I could decide. I had no choice but to 'man-up' and get on with it. What I found particularly hard was having the conversation in the funeral director's office about what Eddie would wear. My eyes welled up. I had my son with me and my friend parked outside in the car, yet I felt so alone. There were all these different options for the order of service to go through, a brochure of the coffins available and everything else in between that you don't want to touch to avoid soiling your hands with reality.

I left that hour's meeting feeling totally drained. On my way home I received a phone call from an aunt of Eddie's in Sierra Leone. She was the other aunty who had come to see us after we had our daughter. Getting straight to the point, she told me she was aware of the problems that certain members of the family were creating. She had received word there was an issue with Eddie's brother and Eddie's cousin's wife, whom I had told where to go a little while before. My aunty asked what had happened and I did not hesitate to tell her.

***

Another relative of Eddie's had been at my house with her husband to offer some moral support and company when Eddie's cousin's wife called. The cousin informed her she was at my house, yet she refused to say hello when asked. Basically, she was just acting up. Eventually she agreed to greet me. I took the phone and was half-stunned into silence at the speed with which she was able to put on a fake voice of concern.

"Hello Dilys. Sorry for your loss."

Bear in mind this conversation was taking place well over a week after Eddie had passed away. I couldn't help myself; well actually I could but I didn't want to. Whatever filter I had with my mouth vanished the day my husband died and even before that it would go missing occasionally.

"What took you so long?" I asked.

"We couldn't get hold of you and you weren't answering your phone," was the best she could do.

I let her have it from both barrels in my finest Krio and told her exactly where she could go with that ridiculous defence all the troublemakers were using to justify the meetings behind my back. She was another one that had always been funny with me but my interaction with her was fairly limited, so she really was quite irrelevant.

She had made the mistake of raising her voice when speaking to me to justify why she hadn't called earlier and I was having none of it. I thought, *I can't stand you either. You're a hypocrite and a fool considering you too have married into this family. If anything happens to your husband, guaranteed, you'll be in exactly the same position as moi!* So that little revelation had me tell her where to stick her condolences and not to bother to come to the funeral. If she did, her and the other misfits who were having meetings about me and trying to make my life hell would be removed by the security personnel I was hiring to manage the numbers and any undesirables. I felt bloody amazing after that little outburst. I thought, *Let me offload some of this crap onto you lot! I have enough weight on my shoulders. Here! Catch!*

I found doing a little of that throw-and-catch technique really helped me. I was able to unburden myself by releasing whatever was thrown my way. By batting things back in the court of those seeking to offend, I could walk away without feeling bitter or remaining angry. It was a weird sort of therapy, but it worked for me. I couldn't hold the kind of emotions I had in. It was interesting because some people had an expectation for me to be this textbook widow, sitting all morose and unable to string a sentence together. They thought my grief made me the perfect candidate to be victimised and bullied but I don't do vulnerable if it means I'm going to be taken advantage of.

So, Eddie's aunt had her work cut out for her, trying to be arbitrator for me and the rest of 'the outlaws'. She asked me if I would be willing to have her attend the funeral as well as Eddie's brother; by now this was around ten days since Eddie's death and quite frankly, I'd had enough. My children were complaining they couldn't grieve because of everything that was going on. I wasn't sleeping and was in such a dark place. However, the one thing I did not want under any circumstances was anyone at that funeral who had disrespected me, my husband or my children to show up. I had people trolling me on social media, outlaws (I refuse to call that group of people my in-laws to tarnish the amazing relatives of my husband who were really there for me) besmirching my name. Meanwhile, I was supposed to 'give it to God' and 'move on' because I was 'better than that and a bigger person'. I wasn't going to give it to anybody; I couldn't move on from something that was still happening and indeed, I was better than that. I was a wife and mother that had lost her husband suddenly and painfully and should never have been treated the way I had, especially in front of my children.

I told Eddie's aunty that the one person who could convince me to relent and allow these people to come to the funeral had not yet been born! With that she laughed and said I was too much like her and that she understood my sentiments. For me it was very simple – you don't put someone through a living hell within 48 hours of their husband's passing then pretend you're remorseful only because the tactics you used to dictate the state of play had woefully backfired. I was nobody's fool and I knew if they attended the funeral, I couldn't guarantee they would be respectful to my husband's memory. For that reason, as Alan Sugar famously says, "You're fired!"

Eventually, it was time for closure on all that was going on. I felt enough attention had been averted from our mourning and it was time to be in the now, as hard as that was. It was time to be present and be in that space. Family and real friends continued to rally round, helping where they could. The kindness shown to me was astounding. I had never seen anything like it before in my whole life. People I didn't know were talking about how my loss had touched them and they were proud of the work I had done for others, so they wanted to give me money in return. I had others offering all sorts for

Chapter 9. Over the Rainbow

the funeral: food, decorating of the hall, providing chair covers from Germany – that was Eddie's niece. One of my friend's husbands took over the details needed for the order of service as they own a photo printing company. I cannot possibly list all the things done for my family but all I knew was that I had never experienced such an outpouring of love and support.

Eddie had been an usher at our old church and all the ushers that could make it to the funeral promised to be there to give whatever help they could. The church I chose for Eddie's funeral had a female vicar – a small thing – but it reminded me of our wedding. I always smile when I see women in positions that you wouldn't typically find them; I notice little things like that, and it gladdens my heart.

It was a bit of a mission to coordinate the church service and the burial as well as finding a hall for the reception to all fall on the same day. Typically, Ghanaians will have the funeral on one day and the reception on another. I don't think people could appreciate how the whole planning process of the funeral made me feel. Frankly, I couldn't wait to get it over and done with. I hated it, I resented it and I despised it. As we planned it, it felt unbelievable. Many a time I had to repeat these words silently to myself because I couldn't get my head around it. *Is he really gone? Eddie? Wow…this wasn't a bad dream after all.* A date was set for Thursday 21 February 2019. As I type this, I can feel the disbelief of what that day was going to mean for the rest of my life. My eyes well up with tears at being taken back to that place.

★★★

The funeral director was so patient with me – a kind soul that treated me so gently, as if I was a family member more than a client. He was going on holiday and put me in the hands of his second in command, a lovely lady who made me a lovely cup of tea when I went to discuss more funeral arrangements. By this time, I'd decided that I was going to dress Eddie in blue – a blue suit and a blue shirt because blue was his favourite colour. Our daughter had also asked that I bury her father in that colour because she wanted to wear blue too with her brothers. I couldn't think of anything more comforting for her as everyone else was being asked to wear black. I didn't do what many people often do and ask people to wear something colourful to celebrate the life of their loved one. No. Everyone was to wear black and be as miserable as me. There was nothing to celebrate. I wanted everyone to feel what I was feeling, and that's the truth. I wanted everyone to feel the pain of what I was having to endure.

"Dilys, we will have Eddie here for you on Tuesday if you want to come and see him."

I'd been waiting for that call since I lost Eddie. He had passed away suddenly so the coroner had to be involved. I was upset because the day Eddie died, they'd said I could see him any time I wanted to; however, I hadn't seen him for nearly a month, two days before his funeral. It was the longest time we had been apart since we married. I had been longing to see him for so long I could hardly sleep. When that call came through, meaning that I would get to see Eddie and talk to him and just be with him, I felt a little comfort in my heart.

Chapter 9. Over the Rainbow

My two friends who had been visiting almost daily accompanied me. We walked through the doors of the funeral home but instead of taking a left and sitting in the welcoming waiting area with a hot cup of tea, I was asked to follow the lovely lady in charge to a tiny chapel outside the main building. I went in with one of my friends because she thought I might need the support but would leave if I needed time alone.

Eddie was in a small room, the third on the right if my memory serves me correctly. I opened the door slowly, took a deep breath and walked inside with my friend in tow. She gently closed the door behind me. I looked down into this beautiful, shiny coffin my husband lay in, in the clothes I had so carefully chosen for him. The lady commented on how stylish my husband must have been, being most impressed with his psychedelic socks when I had taken his clothes to her a few days before. I had proudly proceeded to tell her what an impeccable man my husband was, how he always smelt divine…now here he was, lifeless.

I looked into the coffin and nearly collapsed on seeing him. If it weren't for a pair of very quick outstretched hands that broke my fall, I would have been in a heap on the floor. I couldn't breathe properly, my chest hurt, and I felt cheated. The man lying there wasn't my husband; it just wasn't him. He looked like him somewhat but that wasn't my husband. My husband had gone. He had gone before I could really say goodbye.

"That's not him! That's not Eddie. I'm not coming back here again. I don't want to see him. That's not Eddie…," I managed to say between my sobs.

I was in such a highly distressed state that I was ushered out of the room and straight to the waiting car. I sat in the front seat and stared out of the window for the entire 30-minute journey back home, not saying a single word. Something happened to me when I walked into that room, something I hadn't expected. Whatever it was though, that something helped me immensely in preparation for my husband's funeral.

★★★

The day I lost Eddie, I sat with him in the hospital for hours. I held his hand. I kissed his face. I rubbed his head. I ran my hands over his chest. I laid my head on his chest. I took in everything that I possibly could so I wouldn't forget what he felt like.

I consciously savoured and stored those feelings in my soul so I would remember, and when I needed to, I could go back to that place. I took in the smile he had on his face – so peaceful and so gentle and so handsome. I took it all in.

This was not the man I had just seen and therefore I was able after processing that painful encounter, to accept that my husband was no more. It didn't take much to tell me that I was so fortunate to have seen him before the funeral. Why? Because if the man I saw was the smiling, warm and peaceful man I had sat beside for hours and hours asking why he had left me so suddenly at the hospital on the day he passed away, I wouldn't have been able to bury him. I know without a shadow of a doubt, I wouldn't have been able to go through with it. Somehow, I felt a disconnect and the reality of Eddie being gone and me being on my own was stark. It hit me between the eyes in a way that denial was now impossible.

We were very close. He was so alive. He was so present. The contrast of what was and what is was just too great for me to remain in a state of shock or indeed, denial. I had two children that had lost their father and I couldn't allow them to feel for a minute that the roles had reversed and that they were responsible for me. So, this strength everyone spoke about had to be used to support my children. At the very least, I had to make sure that on the day I didn't crumble. I had to reach so far within myself to be a pillar for them to lean on. I was now so eager for the day to come so I could get it over with. For the next two days I held my breath and focused on that fact that if we got through it, then I would exhale.

Chapter 10

A Kiss Goodnight

Thursday 21 February 2019. The day was finally here. I showered and sat on my bed for a while, thankful the day was here, but so afraid that it was. Eventually I got up to search for a comb because the last time a comb or brush had come near my hair was the day Eddie died. I'd been wearing a black scarf for that whole time. My clothes were prepared the night before. I had a very simple black dress; I didn't want to wear traditional attire to the church because I know my husband wouldn't have wanted me to. I had purchased the largest black hat I could find, something that covered half my face. It took me an age to find the hat but I was very clear in my mind that was what I wanted. Eventually I'd found a milliner in America who was able to get the hat finished in time to ship it over to me.

One might have thought that I had bought a grand hat for attention. The truth was I abhorred the role I had to play. I resented it and hated it. I was angry at being the one who had to do this and, more to the point, at becoming the centre of attention for all the wrong reasons. It's something I felt so uncomfortable about because I had always been and still am fiercely precious and protective of my outward emotions. I felt it such a rude intrusion for my tears, my grief and my pain to be on display like a pay-per-view boxing match on Sky Sports. I was overwhelmed by how sorry people felt for me though I was grateful for their sympathy. As I got lost in the emotions of everyone's sympathy, I no longer felt like myself. I was just the lady who had lost her husband, the lady everyone pitied. Dilys had disappeared.

I managed to put on some make-up, tied my hair in a ponytail, slipped on my dress, a black pair of tights and put on a pair of high, black patent shoes. I finished my attire with a black satin jacket Eddie had bought me many years before. The hat went on and was pulled as far down as it could go to hide my tired, puffy, big red eyes. Not satisfied with how much I was hiding, I donned my black Versace shades, so I was able to hide all I wanted from the world. A black scarf, more for comfort than for warmth, accompanied me as I left the house with my parents, siblings, children, godparents of my daughter and some very close friends and their children.

***

I felt restless as we stood outside. The funeral parlour said they would bring Eddie home so we could leave together for the church. They arrived on time with my darling husband. We had made a kente cloth to be draped over the casket. The kente cloth is usually worn for very special or very important occasions. This wasn't the kind of special I wanted but a cloth often reserved for kings couldn't have been more befitting for my king. I had asked that the cloth be woven in the colours of the Sierra Leonean flag with a touch of gold to symbolise exactly what he meant to us – a man of gold.

Chapter 10. A Kiss Goodnight

After draping the casket, I took my seat in the back of the limousine with my father and elder brother, while my mother sat in the front seat of the car with her grandchildren. A convoy of cars proceeded to make the long drive to the church. *So today*, I thought, *is really happening? It's not a dream after all.* When we got to the church as arranged, I chose to sit with my family first before Eddie was brought into the church. Truth is, I didn't trust myself to stand for that long.

All those years ago, I'd walked down the aisle to the beautiful sound of 'Ave Maria', while Eddie waited at the altar a bag of nerves; now it was my turn to return the honour. I looked back to find the church was heaving with people. That warmed my heart warm, knowing that Eddie was loved so much – it made me feel less alone on this journey of grief. I sat beside my mother who was beside my father with my daughter to my right and my son beside her. I bowed my head as I saw the pall-bearers expertly position the coffin. On top of it was placed a beautiful picture of him, taken at a surprise birthday I had thrown for him years before, smiling that smile.

I bowed my head and grabbed my daughter around her shoulders. I felt so much for her. To lose your dad having just turned 12 was so unjust. My son was having a hard time too, but he felt such a sense of responsibility that he never really wanted me to see him cry.

★★★

A few days after Eddie passed away, I had frantically looked for his wedding band. Eddie wouldn't typically wear his wedding ring at home so would put it in the corner of the chair he usually sat in. We had cleared the living room to make way for the mourners that came to visit but my son had no recollection of seeing the ring. I had decided I wanted Eddie to be buried with his ring so finding it was imperative. I knew he wouldn't usually be without it, so we needed to find it and time was against us. I was so fragile at the time that the thought of not knowing where such an important item was broke my heart. There didn't seem to be any joy finding the ring, so I prayed.

> *Lord, you've taken the most precious thing from me.*
> *Let me find this ring so I can have some joy.*
> *I don't know how I will find it in this big house.*

Two days before the funeral, I heard an almighty "Oh my God! Yes, yes!" I was shaken by the sheer volume of my son's voice and him rushing down the stairs like a bat out of hell.

"Mum I found it! I found it! Oh my God!"

Then he slid down the wall in our kitchen and wept like I'd never seen my son weep before. I just held him while I felt his heart break through those tears. When his sobs settled, I asked him where he'd found the ring and he said I wouldn't believe it. He said he thought his dad must have placed the ring where he found it on purpose. Eddie never went into our son's room for anything, so finding the ring in the back of my son's wardrobe, in a pair of black shorts he had not worn for a long time was beyond baffling. It was even more so because Eddie used crutches and wouldn't have been able to balance himself to place the shorts where they were in the manner they had been found.

I couldn't believe what I was seeing and hearing but a sense of pure relief and gratitude engulfed me. I took the ring and placed it on a chain Eddie had had made, with our

Chapter 10. A Kiss Goodnight

initials – E and D – overlapping each other. He would always deny they were our initials to wind me up, saying it was just the abbreviation of his name. Another strange thing happened when I placed the ring around my neck; I knew instinctively at that point he wanted me to have it and not to leave it with him. It was a piece of him he was giving me permission to keep and I was grateful for that and the peace it brought.

So, this son of mine was a source of all things great and his love for and protectiveness towards me was a beautiful thing to have to rely on. My nephew was also an amazing support – bringing me cups of tea and tending to any need I had. The two of them were more like brothers so during the service, when they both looked at each other and nodded their heads after one of Eddie's cousins whispered in his ear, I knew something was up. The boys got up and left the church for a short while. I wasn't told at that point what had transpired but based on the expression on my son's face, I knew Eddie's brother must have turned up. I reached over and squeezed his hand to settle him. I didn't want anything to take away from the moment. We had had so much to deal with over the past month, I was determined the day would be about Eddie and Eddie alone. I looked behind me again and whispered to myself, "Eddie this is all for you." I felt so supported and felt so much love and grief being poured out for the wonderful soul that was my husband.

Our daughter had written a poem for her father, but she wasn't able to read it so asked her brother. He did a great job, considering he was hurting so badly himself. I was proud of the children. They showed such strength and dignity. I was truly proud indeed and Eddie would have been too.

Chapter 11

Gone But Not Forgotten

Sun, sky, sea and land
Anything, so that we could walk hand in hand
Despising the days that I may have taken for granted
When you were in pain, distressed and lethargic
Positive, loving, humorous and ambitious
Not a bone in his body was truly cruel or malicious
Fathers should love, which he did with a passion
He'll never disappear, I cannot imagine
A football fanatic, knowledgeable and smart
One of the Liverpool fans who spoke from their heart
Football on TV, his computer and phone
But just like the Liverpool slogan, he'll never walk alone
Wife and brother, father and son
United we stand, powerful as one
Daddy was benevolent, affectionate and family proud
No chance he'd leave his closest, even to go up in the clouds
Thoughts, emotions, actions and words
My life, full of sorrow has hit a kerb
I cannot awaken you to see your beautiful smile again
I'll – we'll promise to prosper, because thy soul isn't dead

It was now my turn to stand up and speak about the man I thought I was going to spend the rest of my life with. My mother was concerned about me and asked if I wanted one of my sisters to read my tribute. I felt a little upset she would suggest that, because I thought it was the least I could do in his memory. Only I could convey the message I wanted everyone to hear. The strength I had regained after seeing Eddie two days before fuelled me through that day. It reminded me of the beautiful broken vessels put back together with gold. Although you still see the cracks, they create a different kind of wholeness, and that visit had largely done that to me. I'm broken but woven together with gold to make me a new woman, to carry on the rest of my life in a way that's both painful but beautiful in its own way.

The vicar went on to the next item on the order of service.

"And now, a tribute by Dilys Sillah, Eddie's wife."

I got up, head bowed and still hidden by my black, wide-brimmed hat and dark shades. I had asked my older brother and son to stand beside me for support; in the absence of my husband, they were the first two men that came to mind though my younger brother would have also done a sterling job in supporting his big sister. He had already done his bit when he stood beside Eddie on the day Eddie married me.

My son squeezed my hand and led me onto the podium to speak. I stood there for maybe a minute, breathing long and hard, trying to focus. I had no intention of stumbling over my words. I had no intention of not being able to deliver my last message to my husband and our loved ones. I had no intention of letting Eddie down after I had come so far in trying to make him proud.

Chapter 11. Gone But Not Forgotten

"Eddie was my husband. It's difficult to see anything past that fact. We were together for nearly 17 years and I loved him. I was a friend, a protector, a wife who lived every facet of my marital vows to him, especially the 'in sickness and in health' part over the past nearly four years. I cared deeply for him and about him and that will never change as long as I have breath. We were a double act. Dilys & Eddie. That's what it was and that is what it shall always be.

"I met my husband at work in 2002. The day he met me he told his work colleagues he was going to marry me. He told a Sierra Leonean friend of his that worked in the same office, "Patient dog eat fat bone", meaning one needed to exercise patience to get the best or what one wanted, and he did.

"I went to work not to look for a soulmate but that is what I found. My only regret is that he didn't wait around long enough for us to live our lives together into our old age. I always told him that I couldn't wait for him to grow old because I knew he would look more handsome and distinguished with a grey moustache and beard.

He was different from other people. A totally unselfish character who was completely generous and giving of himself to anyone without exception. He would take me anywhere I needed to go, support my dreams and endeavours and was hugely proud of me. There's little I wanted to do that wouldn't be supported by him. When I decided to go into charity work – supporting victims of abuse – he would often record programmes on TV for me or send me newspaper clippings to my phone so I wouldn't miss anything. He himself became an advocate for women and girls in a way that made me proud to have a husband that could relate on such a deep level to the sufferings of others that he didn't even know.

"He loved me more than I realised and the depth of that love demonstrated over the years in so many ways.

"Eddie was known for his smile, that smile that could light up a room and that charming personality that could draw anyone to him. One of the things I loved about him was his exceptionally quick wit and brilliant sense of humour. He was a fountain of knowledge on any subject and I often asked him why he didn't teach, but he would laugh and say he didn't have the patience. We could sit for hours talking and exchanging ideas and points of view, sometimes much to his irritation, because the truth is, he often knew a lot more than I did on the topics we debated. Of course, I never, ever told him that!

"I never really needed to listen to the news. Eddie was the news. Eddie was CNN, BBC, Sky News, all rolled into one and I loved listening to his take on current affairs.

Eddie loved football and was a passionate Liverpool fan. This proved to be his saving grace when he came into my family because my father, brother, son and most of the cooler members of my family support Liverpool. I would often tell Eddie off for turning our only daughter into a football hooligan for the love and passion he infected her with for the game. It was the only time he wouldn't tell her off for not going to bed on time during the week. Weekends in our house were filled with hours of football on TV with the two or three of them watching games and discussing things that went over my head.

"He loved his daughter. She looks so much like her Papa and I know he would have stuck around for her if he could. He was a great father who loved his children and wanted nothing but the best for them. Eddie believed in the opportunities that education brings, and he encouraged Isobel to do her best, and she did.

Chapter 11. Gone But Not Forgotten

"The essence of the man called Eddie is what I will miss. Everything about this complex-yet-simple man was only just being discovered and now I will only have 'what ifs' to complete the thoughts I am left with for the next chapter of our journey I was embarking on with him. We had only just begun. We were just about to live. We were just about getting it right. We were just about to love each other deeper and longer…and then you left me.

"I never once complained about taking care of him. Not to anyone and not silently in my heart. If I had been asked by God to take my Eddie's pain for him to live, I would have gladly done so in a heartbeat. But He didn't. I wasn't tired. I had another 17 years and another 17 years and another 17 years after that to give Eddie if that is what it took. I wasn't tired.

"Apparently love conquers all but it couldn't conquer the events of the morning of Monday 21 January 2019 to keep my husband and my best friend here with me. I'm grateful for the privilege of knowing him; the beauty of being loved completely by him; the grace to have been the one chosen to look after him and the honour of him asking me to pray and lay beside him during the last moments of his life. The life I was supposed to share with him for many more years to come.

"Eddie, you have broken my heart. I will not pretend that I can be strong because you would have wanted me to be. For once I will be selfish. This is not what I wanted, and the devastation will not go away any time soon. I am not strong, and I don't want to be.

"I will always love you as you loved me, and I will always miss you. I will never forget you. You made me the woman I am today. I thank you. I remain for our children until we meet again. If there is a small window in heaven that will allow you to wave at me some *time through the breeze and through the skies, please do...I will be waiting, and I will be watching.*

"Bye-bye Baby."

By the sheer grace of God, I managed to speak without breaking down save but for a few moments in between. I felt slightly faint and weak at the end, but my two new protectors held me and led me back to take my seat and sing our last hymn.

★★★

Eddie was escorted out of the church to a song called 'Differences' by the American artist Ginuwine. It's the song we had played for our first dance many years before. I remember we spent a whole weekend going through a load of songs to find one that was the right fit. When Eddie heard the words to this song he'd said, "This is it!" The words were so beautiful that I didn't raise any objections and thinking about our first dance now and Eddie's 'performance' on the dance floor is a fond memory to cherish. At the same time hearing the song and seeing my brother and other pall-bearers hoist his casket onto their shoulders gave me a searing pain in my heart. Our life had really come to this and I still couldn't believe it.

We left the church with my head still bowed. I was appointed someone to take me through the crowds of people, not because I didn't want to acknowledge anyone, but I genuinely didn't have the strength to speak. I was not prepared for what I saw outside the church; there must have been at least another 200 people outside, spilling onto both sides of the pavement. I saw faces I hadn't seen in many, many years. People mouthed words of support, encouragement and condolences to me before I was ushered into the waiting car ready to take me to the cemetery.

Again, traditionally in my culture, the widow doesn't go to the graveside. This was something that I wasn't going to raise any objections to. I very rarely go to burials because I find them too distressing and I end up with a migraine for days. So, I gratefully sat in the back of the large limousine watching a wave of people stand by where my husband was to be buried while hymns were sung. It was an amazing day because the sun shone so, so beautifully. I had never known a February morning to be so beautiful.

The funeral director had asked for a rough estimate of graveside mourners as there was only a certain number that could be accommodated. There would be other mourners visiting their loved ones too. I thought there would be roughly about 100 mourners but there turned out to be over 200; some had to be turned away. One person, Eddie's brother, slipped through the net. It was confirmed he had come to the church and was spotted by one of their aunties. She was furious as she had been privy to much of what had been done to us. Security was immediately notified, and he was asked to leave the church. There had been so much outward hostility that I knew their presence would distress my children when we had been put through enough already. I was so protective of my daughter especially and really didn't want anything in the slightest to compound her grief on the day she was bidding her father farewell.

One would have thought that being asked to leave the church would have deterred anyone from coming to the cemetery but alas, that was not the case. I had asked that the security guards go to the reception to ensure guests were taken care of and seating sorted as we clearly had more people than we had anticipated. They disagreed and insisted on having just one doorman at the reception and the rest at the cemetery. I saw the wisdom in their decision when I saw the familiar figure and his wife, accompanied by two others. It was the same aunt who had spotted him in the church that raised her objections to having him place flowers on Eddie's casket. I would have felt completely lost it if that had happened; to me, that would have been akin to him spitting on my husband's grave. It was interesting how he could move heaven and earth to be at the burial of his brother but quite content to leave him to rot while he was in hospital and needed him the most.

Grief really does shine a light on the hearts and minds of those around you. You can be as blind as you want to be, but the truth will slap you in the face; I saw the best and the worst of people during this time. You learn to toughen up from what you're exposed to – it's either sink or swim. I chose to swim and to employ a few swimming styles for good measure.

With approximately 600 people at the funeral and reception, there was always going to be an issue of fake mourners but it didn't bother me. The hardest part had been done and we could wave Eddie off with nothing but pride. Everything came together in ways that were nothing short of divine with even strangers making pledges and showing a level of kindness and selflessness that astounded me. Human beings can sometimes really surprise you and this time it was for good reasons.

Chapter 11. Gone But Not Forgotten

Much has been said about the outlaws, but my in-laws – the *real* relatives of Eddie – were a pillar and a rock to my children and me. All those to whom the outlaws had reported me to in Sierra Leone had never met me but after seeing the way I had been treated, they would call to check on my children and see how we were all faring. Cousins of Eddie's flew in from America to mourn with us and offer support. Others who were here and not a part of the lynch mob would be on the phone to me until the early hours of the morning just consoling me and often just listening to my sobs after the children had gone to bed. They were the real family of Eddie Sillah and I thank them from the depths of my heart for honouring my husband and taking care of me.

Eddie's big sister and her daughter are the ones whose kindness really touched my heart. His sister had always been a woman of class and integrity and she loved Eddie greatly. We were recipients of that love too and that never changed. I'm so thankful for the love and the virtual embrace I allowed to envelop me during those dark hours that continued after the funeral. She herself had lost her husband only three years before; she felt my pain in more ways than one.

***

The period after the funeral proved a lot more difficult than I thought. I was so exhausted I decided to take a trip to Ghana, away from everyone and everything. I left first to prepare for my children's coming and that worked out fine for us. A few days on my own, three weeks with them and then a few more days alone as my daughter had to return to school put us all in a much better headspace.

Nobody could change what happened to my Eddie but there were many very gracious people who helped me to say, "In spite of it all …." They helped me breathe again to officially start my life alone and navigate the healing process with my family and how I would attempt to live life alone.

Chapter 12

The Incoherence of Grief

Nobody prepares you for what grief really is and what it really means. We have so many clichés and an array of opinions and sets of rules we impose on the person who has suffered the loss that it makes it nigh impossible to grieve authentically. Often, we are forced to put on various masks and shows of strength and pretend we are coping. If you're British, it's the old 'stiff upper lip' rhetoric at play and if you're from my part of town it's, 'God knows best' and, 'It is well'. Really?

What I found particularly infuriating was the audacity of spectators of my grief telling those of us who mourn how we should mourn and for how long we should let our tears flow. It is so damaging to our mental and emotional health to place a stop clock on grief when you consider not only the different stages of grief, but also the person's personality, character and the relationship they had with the person who has passed away.

How each individual person deals with their loss is as unique as their DNA; no two people grieve in the same way. The problem arises when one person feels that because they have suffered a loss and dealt with it in a particular way, they are now an authority on how all grief must be dealt with. Worst still are those who have suffered no loss at all but proceed to tell you how to manage one of the most devastating things that could ever happen to a person.

One of the things that has helped me on my healing journey was being totally in control, unwavering and uncompromising in how I wanted my grief journey and healing process to proceed. I guess, to a degree, I was brave in not allowing myself to be 'bullied' into placing my grief into anyone's tidy, cute little dignified box. I said in the very beginning that I wouldn't allow anyone to do that to me and I would do a Frank Sinatra if it came down to it. Nobody advised me to embrace every emotion that I felt – that was entirely my choice. It was both scary, painful and hard.

My philosophy was really quite simple: I didn't want any emotion that I had suppressed, for whatever reason, to come back and bite me when I least expected it. I rode the wave of pain, just like you do contractions in labour. The pain came and it was intense, then it passed; it would be followed by a little respite – a little reprieve – then the next contraction would hit, and I'd do it all again. Dealing with grief was like that for me.

I didn't want to have any horrible surprises after lulling myself into a false sense of security by believing I was okay and had been 'healed'. The truth is you never heal from grief. You learn to cope and manage the emotion in a manner that allows you to still enjoy your life in a way that is meaningful but different from how you lived it before. I have explained this point many times by means of an analogy and this is what

Chapter 12. The Incoherence of Grief

I have shared and understood about what it means to heal. I have a cut and a sore or scar develops over that cut. Despite that, when someone touches it, I feel pain, and so it's fair to say that it hasn't fully healed right? I would still wince if it was scraped or scratched; it may not bleed like it initially did but there would still be pain. I assume you can only be deemed to have healed if when you remember who you have lost, the memory is free from pain and sadness. Of course, it may not be with the same intensity as when the loss first occurred, but many of us have the rest of our lives waiting in anticipation of when grief will hit again.

I remember within a few days of Eddie's passing, my daughter asked me who would give her away on her wedding day. A wave of indescribable sadness swept over me because I knew, at that point, I had another possibly fifteen to twenty years to anticipate both the joy and sadness I will feel on that day. Whoever would be giving my daughter away wouldn't be her father, Eddie. There will be more occasions that will press against that cut to remind me it's there. That is why you can never forget the loss of a loved one and 'move on'. I like to call it 'moving forward', because you are just putting one foot in front of the other to get to a destination, often unknown.

Coping with grief is a journey and every journey has a specific mode of transport. Whatever mode we use is down to either choice or circumstance. I describe my journey as being one with a massive backpack on my back, symbolic of my grief, embarking on this trip that I didn't quite plan. As I walk (I'm still on the journey so I cannot use the past tense), the backpack gets somewhat lighter because the things its contents such as food and water, books, whatever I need, will be used as and when, and will invariably lighten the load. In the same vein emotions such as anger, denial and sadness are all the things in our grief backpack that need to be used and discarded to lighten our load. The backpack might even get light enough to fling over my shoulder. It's not a journey that should ever be rushed or forced because it will do untold damage to the mental and emotional well-being of the person mourning.

★★★

We live in times where everything is quick and easy and where we want instant results. This modern-day attitude is being applied to how we grieve.

'It's been six months. Surely you must be over it by now?'

'Life goes on!'

I find it so cold and callous that anyone would feel that it was that easy to get over it. Loving someone and losing them doesn't work like that. To be honest, even when you don't love someone such as an estranged parent or even an unknown parent and they die and you didn't have time to reconcile or even meet them, that can still have a profound effect on your emotions. People may not understand how you feel or how the death has impacted you but that doesn't make the loss any less bearable. Like I said, grief is an incoherent emotion.

I think that as a society we need to educate ourselves more about the one thing we will all face without exception. We are so ill-prepared for the inevitability of death. Yes, you're right to ask the question – how much can one prepare for death? I will not lie and be like the masses pretending there is a microwave version of overcoming grief; if there was, I would bottle it and sell it, but not before getting drunk on the stuff myself.

Chapter 12. The Incoherence of Grief

The reality is we can be better prepared by covering the basics and much of it is in just being human – showing kindness, compassion, genuine love and concern for starters. We don't need to go to a special school to learn these things behaviours; we should be practising these daily so that those who feel so abandoned after losing a loved one wouldn't feel this way. The friends that once called stop bothering because they were fed up of hearing you sobbing down the phone. On the other hand, there are those mourners who pretend they're fine and dandy after being bereaved so as not to put friends off from coming around.

I personally find it so odd when I hear phrases like, 'I don't know what to say' in the context of not reaching out and supporting someone who is grieving. The truth is, there is nothing you can say to bring the person back. It's okay, we know you don't have the answers. We aren't expecting any; however, it would be nice to just say, 'I'm here for you if you need me,' and mean it. We aren't looking for quotations from The Bible or big philosophical revelations at a time like this; you can just be silent sometimes. It's okay not to know what to say.

It's a shame that it's only when death hits that we scramble around to find ways to support those in mourning. We have many books and loads of information on weight loss, how to heal a broken heart, fitness and health and more but little on how to deal with grief and death. Yet, according to the Office for National Statistics, there were a reported 533,253 registered deaths in England and Wales in 2017, so death is hardly an infrequent event!

It's generally said there are five stages of grief. From my own experience I can tell you they don't follow any particular order and you can even skip some of these stages. For example, I don't believe I ever really went through the stage of anger. Of course, some things angered me but I was never angry at God or Eddie for finding myself in the cold embrace of widowhood. In my book, grief is a rollercoaster of emotions that show up uninvited when you least expect it and with no respect for whether it's convenient to rear its ugly head or not. There was an occasion when I was in Next in the West End shopping for black clothes for my break to Ghana. Whilst standing in the queue, joking with the sales assistant, my daughter called me from her father's phone. His picture popped up and I had to run out of the shop to cry my eyes out in the doorway. See what I mean? Grief has no bloody respect and is so attention-seeking. It's temperamental, disrespectful, inconsiderate, unpredictable and merciless.

Truth is, we don't 'move on'. We just move forward. There is no final destination where we drop our grief off and leave our loved one behind. We take that love and those memories with us for eternity. Time stands still when it comes to our feelings for those we've lost. To force ourselves to fit the ideals of those who have never loved and lost through bereavement is like chasing shadows; we'll never catch them. Don't waste time trying to make a myth happen because it's impossible. Take your steps when your feet are ready to move. Embrace whatever you feel when you feel it and then you'll learn what works for the unique journey you're on and the unique person you loved. Let's walk through the stages.

Acceptance. We go through so many emotions before we reach this stage of the grieving process and let's face it, some people never fully accept their loss. Grief can do horrible things to the mind and emotions hence why it's so dangerous to rush anyone through a process only they can figure out. It must be done their way and by their rules. To try to expedite the process can leave the person feeling alone, desperate, full of doubt and adopting feelings of self-condemnation. None of these are at all healthy or helpful in assisting them to move forward or for their mental health.

The truth is there is no right way to grieve. No template has been given for us to adhere to. As I said earlier, how we grieve is as unique as our DNA, so we need not try to impersonate or mimic someone if that is not how we are genuinely feeling. Therefore, it's important for us to be educated about grief; that means we can be that support that spots the signs of the grieving impersonator. We can then confidently say, "It's okay. You don't have to be strong or pretend you're okay. It's okay if you're finding it hard to accept your loss."

Those grieving often wear a mask for fear of being judged if they are not coping. Unfortunately, that means that outsiders can presume that the bereaved is healed, not take the time to really check that all is well. Understanding grief means that we know to ask how the bereaved really is with a genuine interest in the answer. Being present and silent for that person to speak or to share the silence with them is priceless and so empowering.

It's a blessing to be able to accept the loss of a loved one. However, it can take time to get to this stage. The delay can be for several reasons. The circumstances surrounding the death and the other stages of grief such as denial can all hamper getting to that final stage. This also why when we tell a grieving person that time is a healer, they can feel pressurised when in reality, time being a healer is a fallacy. Accepting the passing of a loved one is where the process of healing can begin but that only comes when it's ready to come.

Denial. I believe there will always be an element of disbelief when a loved one passes away. I don't think it always makes a huge difference if the death was expected or unexpected either. Grief is grief to the person who is left behind. The hallmark phrase of denial, 'I can't believe this has happened to me,' is not unusual and can last for however long it wants to.

Part of this stage of grief is a type of defence mechanism to help a person to take in what has happened and to cope with the overwhelming emotion and magnitude of what has happened. It can help to some degree by allowing for a moment to lose touch with the reality of the loss and process the fact that the person is no longer with us. It's hard to come to terms with seeing someone one minute and then, the next, they're gone.

I remember saying to my son when I had one of my down days that 'forever is a long time.' I just couldn't get my head around sitting down with my husband and having a normal conversation where he was well, in good spirits and me bidding him goodnight, to him being gone forever the following morning. In an instant, my whole life had changed. I remember being offered condolences and thinking what the hell was the person offering them trying to tell me? They couldn't possibly be talking to me even though the conscious part of my brain knew full well that my husband had just died. When I shared this with my son, I wanted him to understand that it had only dawned on me that I would never see Eddie again…ever. That came as a revelation, even though it's plainly obvious that when someone passes away, you're not going to see them again.

As a person of faith, it made it more unbelievable that this was happening. All the things I had prayed for and believed about my present state and my future hadn't in any way made any allowances for this kind of life-changing event. I then questioned absolutely everything I'd ever believed in and started to analyse and dissect the simplest of things because I didn't know what was real and what wasn't. There then comes a fear of believing in anything because you had faith before, and it failed you. You often feel afraid to dare to dream. Death makes you question everything and affects all the things that you once took for granted. You don't know if you'll be around to enjoy them. This is perfectly normal, and you must refuse to condemn yourself for those feelings. You can't make sense of everything at a time like this.

Depression. When the reality of the loss we've suffered sets in, depression can hit pretty hard and quite mercilessly. This is a hard one for me because I have become quite an advocate for those suffering from depression in my community. It's an emotion that is looked on as a weakness. There are general myths about depression in all societies and that is evident from how we identify and treat depression. If depression sets in where there is no event to pinpoint, little or no sympathy or help is given. You're expected to 'snap out of it' or 'pull yourself together' and the truth is everyone who suffers from depression or who has suffered tries to. The thing is depression isn't an emotion that you can fix. It isn't something that can be regulated or controlled by mere willpower.

This part of grief can really take you to the pits. It's like a tsunami – a great and mighty wave of sadness washing over you and drowning everything out, making you feel heavy under its weight. I cannot tell you how long it will last but I can only tell you once you're under the waves, wait until you can come up for air. Then hopefully you can get to and stay on dry land for a while. Our personality can also determine how hard depression hits. As sociable as I am, I'm also very private and insular. I can naturally retreat, not wanting to talk to anyone or see anyone, going into myself to gather my thoughts until I'm ready to see the world. It's difficult for those around me but at the same time, trying to pull me out of that place can be counterproductive. I know what I need to do to self-heal and often just need the time and space to do that. My personality means I will check in with myself and be very much aware of what to do to help to get me back into a healthy, emotionally balanced place.

As a qualified life coach, I used some of the techniques I taught to help me. Creating space for myself to hold a mirror up to my thoughts and feelings helped me cope and identify triggers of grief I knew would need attention. For example, my first birthday without my husband turned out to be awful. I'd had a lovely dinner with friends and family the day before and had a few friends round on my actual birthday. We had so much fun and laughter; nobody would have been prepared for how I felt once the night was over.

I had a friend stay 'round and as we were clearing up the dishes in the kitchen, Eddie's name was mentioned and that left me absolutely bereft. You would never have believed it was the same person hours before, doing impersonations and cracking jokes. That feeling of grief lasted the best part of a week, with me in bed for most of that time. The interesting thing is I was absolutely fine on my anniversary and my husband's birthday, but was so sad on Father's Day; see what I mean about the incoherence and unpredictability of grief?

So, being proactive and analysing my own behaviour, there were two things I discovered: a), I needed to pay attention to how I may feel with the first Christmas and New Year coming up and, b), I needed to have some emotional health support.

Both these revelations had easy solutions for me. I knew I couldn't do Christmas at home, so I needed to be away – booking a holiday took care of that. The additional emotional help came in the form of a counsellor. I had suspected there may have been an element of Post-Traumatic Stress Disorder (PTSD) as I was with my husband when he died so I wanted to ensure I took the best steps to deal with any triggers.

I really believed that my profession came into play when I knew it was time to call it quits on going it alone. There is way too much ignorance and unjustified stigma in looking after one's mental or emotional health and seeking support from a professional. Few of us would have an issue seeing the doctor about a pain in our back, or anywhere else for that matter, but as soon as it comes to the mind or heart, it's suddenly taboo. I cannot stress enough the importance of not waiting until you're rock-bottom before seeking support for grief and depression. There is absolutely no need to suffer and reach the very depths of despair before trying to climb out.

For me, counselling was very helpful; I also ensured the family got the help they needed. It put things into perspective by being in a non-judgemental place where you can talk freely, by being completely honest about where you are without the risk of hurting any feelings or creating any worry. Counselling is the smart way to deal with grief if you are struggling to cope; it makes it a less painful and difficult journey than it needs to be.

Bargaining. We tend to try to bargain our way out of the impending occurrence of death. We plead and beg God not to take our loved one away and try to trade with God or whoever it is we believe has the power to turn the situation around. Promises are made – swearing to be kinder or more loving to the person we want to stay and to make changes in our own lives if only our loved one would be spared. We beg for one last chance to prove we will get it right this time and won't mess things up. This isn't a stage of grief that applied to me at all. I think Eddie's death was all too real and final so I had no opportunity to ask for him to come back. I had to face my harsh reality full-on.

Anger. A lot of people feel angry when a loved one dies. It's difficult to explain this emotion because, again, it doesn't appear to be particularly rational, especially if the anger is directed at the person who has died in circumstances beyond their control. Then there's so much going on in our heads, emotionally and with day-to-day things that still need attention. When anger comes, we can just lash out. It's an outlet that needs to be used if that's how you're feeling. It's totally normal when you consider how much your life is going to change because of your loss.

I didn't feel angry at Eddie, but I guess there was an element of anger that I channelled towards certain situations. That included hearing things like, 'He's in a better place.'

Chapter 12. The Incoherence of Grief

I got so irritated recently when someone said that to me that I promptly asked them, "How do you know? Have you been there before?" Yes, maybe not very gracious of me but when you're constantly being force-fed acceptance and being pacified, I think you're allowed some slip-ups from time to time.

Anger, I have always believed, is a positive emotion; it's what you do with the anger that makes it negative. So, if you are grieving and you need to scream and shout and demand to know why your loved one left you to face life alone, raising kids, sorting out debts, managing family feuds – be angry because you've certainly earned the right. The trick, if ever there was one when dealing with grief, is to try not to dwell there for too long. It really is exhausting.

Chapter 13

Death Respects No Person

Nobody has a monopoly on death and, as such, it's a necessary evil that all who are born will invariably experience. I was ignorant about the trauma I was to suffer at the loss of my husband, the treatment I would be subjected to, the friends who would be there for me and those that wouldn't. To say the whole experience has been an eye-opener is an understatement.

After joining a few bereavement groups and speaking to other widows and people who have suffered loss, I realised something. Contrary to my assumption that my experience was unique and exclusive to women of West African descent, we were all in fact, in the same boat. It's also worth mentioning the cruelty experienced doesn't always come from in-laws – somehow death can bring out the worst in all of us.

I started writing this book with the intention of shedding light on how many African women are treated when their husbands pass away but, very quickly, I came to the realisation that that was not the case. I identified a trend across communities and continents that we all seem to be getting this thing wrong and in my small way, I wanted to once again be that voice that shouts, 'Hey! Look over here. Look what I've found!' That's because I know change is needed but we can't change what we don't know and if through this process, one more widow or family that is bereaved can receive a little kindness, a little compassion, then it would have been worth it.

I asked some of these women who were so poorly treated, why their own families didn't stick up for them and protect them. The shocking answer I received was that some of these people had behaved like that themselves, so understood it was a cycle that all widows had to go through. It then becomes a 'wait your turn' scenario and a rite of passage that is assumed to be the way for every widow.

You will now read the accounts of four very special women who suffered loss of loved ones. Three are widows and one is the adult child of a widow who also went through a divorce. Their stories are real and their experiences heart-breaking, and for this reason, their stories are told verbatim with no editing. Afi, Penelope and Rachel are African women and Anne is an American. I hope their experiences will encourage us to hold those who are suffering loss gingerly in the palms of ours hands, give them abundant love, care and patience and so help them carry their backpacks along their journeys to coming to terms with their loss.

Chapter 14

Afi's Story

My name is Afi and I'm 36 years. I lost my husband eight years ago. It hasn't been easy but all I can say is that God has been faithful. His passing away was really a shock because at a tender age, at the age of 27, I had a four-year-old child. He'd been sick on and off with admittance to hospital several times where scans, tests and a whole lot of things were done. Nothing was found so we were just believing in God for a miracle.

That fateful day, when I came back from work and my husband was indoors and complained about his stomach. I was like, "Okay, let's just go to the hospital and have a check." Immediately when we got there, he couldn't even get up from the car to the ward so he was wheeled in. Throughout the night he was crying. His ribs were hurting and a whole lot of doctors were attending to him. He stayed in the hospital for three days. I was the only person taking care of him because everyone else was far away. Our relatives were not around so basically, I was the only with him at the hospital.

So, all he kept telling me was just to be strong, be strong, be strong. I knew he was going to die. There was another patient by his bedside. It was an elderly man who asked if I had anyone around to help me. I'm sure he knew I was struggling. So, I called a member of our church who came. As soon as he came, I went and sat elsewhere to rest. That was around midnight. Within five minutes I went back to the ward. When I got there the man taking care of him was at the entrance of the ward. I asked, "What is going on here? What is he doing here and where is my husband?" He replied that the doctor was taking care of him, so he was waiting outside. I saw them wheeling someone away covered in a blanket, but I didn't see the person. I said, "The guy taking the dead body away was our nurse. He was with us throughout the night, so how come he is taking the body away?" He replied, "Someone just died on the ward. So, they have asked him to take the body away." It was later I found out that my husband was that body.

I went back home. Two days later I was expecting my period which never came. I brought a pregnancy test kit and I did a test. Fortunately, or unfortunately, I was pregnant. I went to the hospital. I know a doctor friend and I told him the situation. I needed an abortion. He said he could do it, but I would have to come back if I really wanted it. So, I left and told the family what had happened, that their son was dead. Even the way they were blasting me on the phone alone was unbearable, so I knew something else was coming.

They came and saw my son and me. He was four and we were in the room with a church member. For three good hours they were sitting outside with church elders. Somebody asked them, "The widow and son are in the room. Have you

Chapter 14. Afi's Story

checked on them to see how they are doing?" They replied they were not there because of me but what they were coming to do was more important. I knew there was a fire on the mountain. They took the body away and left me and his son alone in a strange land. So, I called my daddy and told him what had happened. My daddy called them and told them, "It was your son that took my daughter there. If he is no longer there and you have left her and taken the dead body away, I'll give you three days to bring my daughter."

On the third day they sent someone for us. The person they sent was given instructions not to bring me to the house but for me to go straight to my father. That person was my late husband's cousin. He brought me to my daddy's house. I met my dad, and he said, "We need to go to their house and let them know what happened." I told my dad, "They have already said I should not go to their house." Fortunately, or unfortunately, I had a grand-uncle who was married to my late husband's aunty, so it's like we are all related in a way.

When they had the meeting, the women came to talk to my grand-uncle. My grand-uncle said I was welcome, so I went and stayed with him and my aunty. All this was going on while I kept my pregnancy secret and never told anyone. I was three months gone and I told my grand-dad's wife. She noticed there was a change. I wasn't eating without putting salted fish in any food and when she gave me water to drink, I didn't drink it. She thought I was just unwell. She asked if I had told anyone, and I said no, so she said I should tell my mum, which I did. My mum said she would think about something. My grand-uncle and his wife advised me to tell my mother-in-law that I was pregnant. I went to see her and told her the situation. She was like: "Okay, that is good news." From day one when I first entered her house, she welcomed me up to this very day. She has never left my side and has been a darling and a good woman. I have been telling her that should I live again, I would choose her as my mum-in-law.

The news started flying around that it wasn't even their brother that impregnated me. It was so sad. I kept the baby. By this time the funeral and everything was over. So many things had happened during the funeral but, overall, I was strong. My mother was around, my friends were around, so I had a little comfort and a shoulder to cry on.

I had to go to a house for widowhood rites. I was just kept in a room for three days.

A certain old woman was supposed to be with me throughout. She had to cook for me, bathe me but she made my mum do all that for me. They had the traditional way of doing things but because of Christianity, I wasn't taken through that. The pastor blessed my black cloth for me. That's what I was supposed to wear for three days. I was supposed to bathe before six in the morning and six in the evening. I wasn't allowed to talk to people a lot. They said I would become talkative if I did. All the dresses, the cups and everything I used in that room, including my beads, were taken off. My mum was shown a refuse dump to throw them in. I was made to cut a bit of my hair and my nails as well. The black dress was supposed to be worn for a year but everything changed. I wore mine for three months.

One of my sisters-in-law told me that if I knew it wasn't their brother that impregnated me, I shouldn't go into the room, otherwise I wouldn't go back home again. I told her

Chapter 14. Afi's Story

that I would come back and give her a call. So, they left me and my mum. Incidentally, this particular sister-in-law was trying to take my son away from me. He was four! I was like, "No way. I just lost my husband and you are taking my child away from me too. Why? It's too painful." It became a struggle in the town and the chief in the village sent for us and asked what the issue was. I explained everything to him, and he said they hadn't had a son before so they should wait 'till he was five or ten years old before they take him, but not at this tender age. There was no one around me so it would be too much for me, so they should wait.

After three days, widowhood rites were over. I left to where my late husband and I were still in school. I went to continue my schooling while pregnant and with the little one. My mum came with me. We were living near Sunyani. My mum has been helpful.

I gave birth to the second one, a boy. The day I gave birth, I called my mother-in-law and told her what happened and she was happy. I asked her what name should be given to the child. She said she didn't know. She said I should ask my late husband's siblings and I agreed. I asked and one of them brought a name. Before we came, I told my son I was pregnant. He had been playing with a young boy in the town where we lived and told me to name the baby after that boy. It was no problem as I was already calling him the name before birth. So, we combined the names. The church did a lovely blessing for us, but nobody came from my husband's side of the family to see us. Not even to see if the baby was born or if we survived.

The one year anniversary came and we had to travel down. I took my son and his brother. The baby was almost eight months. We went and they were all looking at the baby whether to carry him or not. After the one year anniversary, I went back to Sunyani to finish school then I relocated back to Accra.

I have been through a lot. I have been fighting depression. It's so traumatic, losing a loved one. It is not an easy thing. At times I'll be in my room and cry. For eight years I have been on medication. Not even my mum or my dad knows about it. Nobody knows. I have been suffering panic attacks, depression, the whole lot. At times I have this feeling I am going to die. I have to take medicine before I can calm myself down. Ideas of suicide and low thoughts go through my mind. I am living for my children. They are the most important things to me now. There was nothing to inherit as we were just young people. We were just starting life so there was nothing to fight for. It has been state benefit and that's all. I was a naïve girl who didn't know anything at the age of 27. I had friends who were way older than me from church, and my mum has been a great support.

I remember in Sunyani I couldn't sleep alone, so I had to move from friend to friend. In the evening, I would call and ask to spend the night. I would put my baby in the car and drive off and we would go and spend the night. So, one day, I got fed up and I decided to sleep at home. I got everything ready and by 6 o'clock we were in bed. Then, all of a sudden, the lights went off. The day I decide to sleep at home then this happens. I had an inner spirit tell me that no matter what, you can do it. Can you imagine I was using my phone torch

Chapter 14. Afi's Story

as a light but around twelve the battery ran down and the phone went off? I couldn't sleep 'till daybreak but was praying continuously that the little ones were okay.

So, when we came down, I gave the big boy to one of my aunties. When the baby was two, he realised his big brother was staying somewhere else so he wanted to go and join him. I took him there too and he stayed with the father's sister for five years. Five long years they stayed with their aunty.

Loneliness set in. I used to cry myself to sleep sometimes, but in all, God has been faithful. He has seen me through. Now I have my children with me so I can say the loneliness is a bit less.

The last three weeks the little one has been asking his big brother where his dad is. His big brother pretended as if he didn't hear him, so he asked again. "Where is my daddy?" So, his big brother replied, "Daddy is Jesus Christ." The little one replied, "Jesus Christ is everyone's daddy, but where is our real daddy?"

I called him and told him his daddy had gone to heaven because he was dead. I was sure, aged seven, he should know what death is. But I am not so sure, as sometimes he asks to go to heaven so we can see him. He is the best thing that ever happened to me. I miss him so much. Every possible moment I wish he was here to see how his boys have turned out. But, hey, we love him, but God loves him more. We just pray that his soul rests in peace until we meet again.

When it comes to the support of the family, they were not there for me when I needed them. Just imagine. I am 27 years old and pregnant when my husband dies. I am accused of infidelity. I gave birth and no member of the family comes to even see the baby for a year, not until I have to go back for the anniversary. That's the first time they saw the baby. I think it's an African or Ghanaian thing. They think it's fair.

I am trying so hard to be free of the panic thing and the depression thing. I am seeing a psychologist every month. I have been seeing him for five years now. He's putting me on drugs and I am trying to take myself off. It hasn't been easy. For the past two months, I think I have tried. I am trying music therapy. I listen to music a lot and use it to get to sleep so when I wake up, I am more relaxed.

Most days, I wish he was still around. I see people and I wish it was us. The big boy is a replica of him. The boys are coming now. I don't want them to see me crying so we will have to continue this another time.

Chapter 15

Rachel's Story

My father died before my mother, but this whole sense of bereavement started long before he died, if that makes sense. My mother was ill, and I think if she lived here, they probably would have labelled her as schizophrenic.

So, throughout childhood, sometimes she was home, sometimes she wasn't, and there was always this stigma in the family. My father, being Dr Phillip and all, had gone and married someone who isn't 'all that', so there was always that ill feeling. So even as a child, he knew his side of the family looked at us differently because his family was from a certain tribe. There were all those little things to it that you don't realise as a child, but you are aware that there are comments made from time to time and you're being set aside for whatever reason. And so, this feeling of abandonment was there a long time ago, even as a child. Sometimes we'd come home from school to no mother because she had been taken away to the mental institution. They wouldn't let us see her. So, you can imagine as a child when you come home and your mother isn't there, how painful that was. Nobody *ever* explained.

I guess they didn't understand her condition let alone how to explain to the children.

All in all, we were three girls and two boys, and I was the youngest. We learnt to look after ourselves very early on. When she was there, sometimes she wasn't really there. There were different layers of wasn't there and you had to learn them quickly, even to interact with her and her different personalities. She could have had split personalities, could've been all those things but, of course, she was never diagnosed. So, growing up I have felt this separation on different levels: psychological, emotional and the rest. It's always been there and this thing about the mother being the caregiver was never really that straightforward for us. The caregiver sometimes became the person you had to care for.

Nobody talked about it. It was almost like this is how it is, but nobody explained to you what it meant, you know, for her, for you, my dad, the rest of them. Nobody ever talked about it. And growing up I noticed every time that it was easier not to talk about it. And so, I've always had this fear. In fact, I know that has even influenced the way I have brought up my own children and that's all the reason why I didn't want to go back to work after I had my daughter. There's something about finishing school and coming home and your mother not being there. That still haunts me...still really haunts me. I didn't realise that it affected my sleep, even as a child, because I was always listening out. Is she coming back? Or listening out for people I call predators, the family members who hover around. Do you know the people I'm talking about? I've always had issues with sleep and I think it goes back to that. You might go to sleep and in the morning she's gone.

Chapter 15. Rachel's Story

So, about this whole thing of not being told. No one thinks it's important enough to sit you down because as far as they are concerned, you're a child. It's almost as if, not that you don't matter, but it felt like that. I remember bringing up my kids and friends would say, "Why are you talking to the child as if they're an adult?" When I was her age, I was already an adult. I came fully-equipped. Just because my size is like that doesn't mean my consciousness is that little. So, I was always aware of that, always, at a very young age. Physical, mental, emotional, spiritual. I understood it all. Nobody helped me to put it together.

When my father died, I was 14. My dad was 49 and he had diabetes-related complications. He went into a coma, never recovered and then died.

Again, the assumption is, you will get by. You're too small to understand what's going on – that's the assumption again – and that when you grow up you won't remember much of what is being said around you. At the time I listened and heard everything. The put-downs that were being said back and forth between the families and the words said towards my mother. My mother wasn't well at that time, so she didn't go to the funeral and that was a big deal for a lot of people. In their eyes, she didn't seem fit to be there. She didn't do what was expected of her, what tradition requires, without them realising, or perhaps they didn't want to consider the fact that she wasn't well enough to be present. My mum must have been in her 40s because she is three years younger than my dad, about my age now. A lot to put up with and I have stopped myself, you know of thinking about her in her position.

You know she's not well enough to look after herself and her children – and her only source is her husband and he dies.

But you know, before my father died – I must backtrack. Before my father died, my older sister died. She was 11 and I was seven. Sickle cell. So again, nobody told us anything. She died and that was it. Nobody thought, bearing in mind how close we were. She was a sister that was closest to me in age. Nobody thought that it would have affected me. And so that was my first experience of loss and again, I don't know how it affected my other siblings but I'm sure everybody had their own story around it.

Again, there's always a blame game going on when someone dies. 'You didn't take good care of her!" Whatever. There's always something and you hear it all, even as a child. You hear it and you think *What does that mean? She did what she could!*

It happens, and rather than us dealing with the issue, there's always a blame or negativity around everybody and everyone, and as a child you hear it, you see it. Yes, your voice doesn't count but it doesn't mean you're stupid. Consciously, you are aware of everything and you're recording it, trying to make sense of it. So, when my father died it was of course a massive upheaval. I think it affected my older brother because he went to Uni and just couldn't concentrate. A few years ago, we talked about it and I realised that he went through a mental breakdown of his own. He was the first son and I think he'd taken it upon himself. He had a lot to show, a lot to prove. He was worried about my mother – whether he was in a good position to even look after my mother. He's not yet a man and yet, you know, he's got these responsibilities. I don't think that anyone ever said to him "You know what, you don't have to feel responsible."

People say all these things without realising the depth of the damage. He was not ready to be a man. It was forced upon him and everyone. There are these expectations. Layers and layers of expectations without ever having to ask what's actually going on with you following what's happened. Nobody actually stops to think. It's almost as if it's a relief for them if they can give you that role so they don't have to think. It feels almost like that.

When my father died, he hadn't made any preparations for how his kids would be looked after or how his wife would be looked after. I believe he had property and other things which his brother knew about but because my mother wasn't well enough, he never told her what he had. She didn't know *anything*. So obviously if there was something there, maybe it could have been used to look after us if we knew about it. It's very characteristic of African marriages but I think it's made worse by the fact that my mother wasn't well. So again, she's sick and therefore nobody needs to tell her anything. She was sick but there were moments where she knew what was going on. She should have known, or she should have been told. It worked to their advantage not to tell.

I remember at my father's funeral, my uncle said that he would look after us. So, they make all these declarations in front of other people knowing very well they can't fulfil them. As a child I heard it all, but their actions meant they had no intention, because if you really wanted to, my brother wouldn't have dropped out of uni. He couldn't support himself. My uncle's own kids were in the same school so he could have helped if he wanted to. My father was very close to that uncle so I'm sure he knew what my father had in terms of property, land and all that, but we never knew.

People appear to be close to you but when the person goes, they completely disappear. It was around that time when we finished the Common Entrance exam. I wanted to go to a particular school, but I couldn't because it was easier for me to stay home since I was a day student. It was better for me to stay home and commute to school so that someone would be home to look after my mother. There was a part of me that resented that. All my brothers were able to go out of town to schools of their choice, but when it got to me – no. But somebody needed to, so I felt compromised. Somebody needed to so then that was it. So anyway, as I was grieving about other things, I didn't even realise what I was grieving about.

And we don't take these things seriously. We don't place any emphasis on emotional or mental health support. You're just expected to try your best. I heard this story of someone who went to the dentist. The dentist did something and the patient was in pain from whatever it was he did. The anaesthetic didn't work. Apparently, the nurse said, "Just be strong, dig deep, just dig deep." If that were me, I would have hit her over the head with whatever I could find, but that kind of sums it up!

So, for a child, you also feel responsible for what happens but you're not responsible for it! I beat myself up forever because I was supposed to go there on Thursday and I thought *Oh, I'll wait for the weekend and then I'll go.* He died on the Friday night. If I had gone on Thursday...nobody knew about that. I spent forever saying, "If I'd gone, he wouldn't have died, and I would have given him something to live for." We were very

Chapter 15. Rachel's Story

close. I couldn't tell anyone about these things. You just need to hear "It's not your fault" or "No, you couldn't have done anything." And it can work wonders. You're not seen. You're just a chess piece. Others are making decisions around you. Nobody's asking. In fact, nobody needs to know what you feel, whether you have any…it doesn't matter.

I think my mother was badly treated by the family. Some members of the family managed to do their bit though. I moved to another area. I moved there as my aunty felt she could look after me so that my mother didn't have to. She did her bit in a way. Looking back, my aunty saved my mother the responsibility of having to worry about me, but then it left her on her own and I felt guilty for that. Do you know what I mean? So, for example, you get a scholarship to go somewhere, but you're sad that you're leaving your mother behind. You'd hope your mother, or somebody would say 'It's okay, I give you permission. It's okay that you're going with my blessing,' but nobody says anything. Those little big things aren't said.

So, when I speak about abandonment, it started when my mum was sick. Different scenarios seem to have reinforced the idea that I had done the abandoning in my child-like mind, as well as me feeling abandoned by the bereavement and by her sickness. How could dad die knowing that mother could not look after us? What did he do that for?

I think my dad's death impacted my mum's mental health. I think she found it very difficult because she went in and out of the mental hospital for longer periods than before. I think she must have gone through her own grief because her illness was such that you had to be mindful of what you ate when she was the one cooking.

My children I talk to a lot. I used to talk to my daughter when she was young like an adult. When she asked me a question, I would tell her the truth because she was the kind of child who would come back and say, "But you said this", so I don't lie to her because there is no need to lie.

The treatment of my mother impacted me. My mother didn't have the capacity to manage her grief as well as mine. I can imagine how it would have made her feel that she wanted to help and but just couldn't. She physically couldn't no matter how hard she tried and that's what mental illness does. You want to do something, but you can't. People tell you to snap out of it. You want to be happy, you want to be emotionally sound and stable but it's deeper than that. It's not like that because mental illness isn't a feeling.

It was almost for me as if I needed permission to grieve too. Permission and reassurance. We all need a safe place to be able to grieve. I think I learnt very early on that you must look within. Not to let them know what's going on because they can't do anything about it. If they haven't figured it out now, then if you feel it, then you deal with it. Those were my thoughts as a child. So now, I deal with a lot of things by shutting myself off. It's nothing to do with anyone. I just figure that I will figure it out because that's always been my coping mechanism. One of the things that got me through some of the experiences was that I knew my father very well, so I would say things and be like, "If I do this, dad will be proud of me". That kind of helped me at every stage. You get to that point and that's where you change what's happened in a way.

Chapter 15. Rachel's Story

Well you can't change it, but you make it a positive thing. That becomes your motivator and your reason for being…in a way.

My experience when my mother died was completely different to when my father died. First, when my mother died, I was an adult. I thought that because I survived my father's death, when my mother died, it wouldn't be so bad because I'd already gone through this. Hell no! It was ten times worse! Because then I realised all the things I'd kind of pushed aside because of her illness. My mother never really knew me because I would keep things away from her in order not to trigger her illness. So again, I had to abandon the 'mother and daughter' role for my survival and hers. There's a lot of things I wouldn't discuss with her and it's because maybe I'd grown up with this 'she won't understand' rhetoric. I also brought into the label placed on her the she was an unwell woman, and even though I knew her as my mum, I couldn't separate that seed that had been planted that had grown. I couldn't tell my mother, even when she was fine because I didn't want to make her worry. *I don't need to tell her* I'd say to myself. Some things she never knew about me and I felt really bad about that. There were times I was facing this woman who when she was fine was very creative and very stylish. Sometimes people would be with her and when they leave, they couldn't understand how anyone would say she was unwell because she would wake up, dress up and be normal. She was a designer and she would be well presented. She looked perfect and yet she wasn't all there.

However, my dad's family were aware of the extent of my mother's mental illness but whether they understood it is another thing. I think for some of them it was convenient not to understand her illness. For others they felt they had to defend because they were close to my dad. Those he was closest to felt they had to do something to protect her and some people did. Generally, I felt that she wasn't taken seriously, and I could see it even from those who were helping. That hurt for a child to see that that's how your mum was treated. I saw her just as my mum, not as someone who is ill, but I had to learn to separate the two – my mum the mentally ill person and my mum. I'm very comfortable with compartmentalising as it works for me. It had always worked for me. It's my go-to thing.

So as a child, I found that if we were talking about grieving, I realised I was grieving for the fact that he left us and shouldn't have. He was also my friend. I think I was grieving for the life I wouldn't have. At that moment in time you see the past and then you automatically look to the future. You see where you are now and immediately are so frightened of the future, You fear what's going to happen. You question your own place because you're half of that somebody and that somebody's gone and you question you. What am I doing here? You question all that. Sometimes a child doesn't have the capacity to articulate but that doesn't mean they don't have the awareness. How do you put it in words so people can understand? If somebody were to have asked, you'd break it down, but nobody asks you.

You know what? I've always had this deep sense of connection and I think one day I had a dream of my dad. I was quite grown but I was sleeping between my mum and my dad. I remember my mum telling my dad that he should stop encouraging me to sleep in their bed because I was 12 and had started my period. My dad would say it was okay because that's how close I was with my dad. I just wanted to be near him. Anyway, I had a dream. He came to see me. He came in a box. He came to visit me. I was so happy. I was like, "Oh my God, I've been dreaming all this time! Now you're here!" He said, "Don't touch me, don't touch me" and I asked him why. He said "I don't want them to know I came to see you, don't touch me. You'll be all right." He kind of tried to encourage me, reassure me. I remember, as he was going, he took some leaves and wiped me with them saying he didn't want 'them' to see that he came and saw me. Then he disappeared. I was 14 when I had that dream. When I woke up, I had urinated on my bed. That's how intense the whole thing was.

The only other time I peed on my bed was when my mother died. A full grown woman like myself. I suffered from insomnia after my mother passed away and I actually had to seek therapy because I couldn't sleep.

I embraced the feelings that I had but you'll be amazed how much catches up with you even later. My divorce brought out some other stuff I didn't realise was there. The one male figure in my life decides to leave me. He didn't die like my father had but he chose to leave me and that woke up something in me. The abandonment hit me for six. I thought I had dealt with it, but it all came back again. My father died. He didn't choose to leave me and there is nothing more painful. I'm not trying to belittle you by saying you don't understand but there's nothing more painful than grieving for the living because the dead have nothing to explain to you. They're gone. You're grieving for the person that you see, yet you're supposed to tell yourself they're dead to you. You're with them and you're coming in and out and you don't have the space to grieve because he's come to see his kids and you're interacting with him.

I spent so much time looking within. It tended to wake up other things that you thought you'd dealt with. I made peace with myself and I realised he didn't leave me. In a way he left himself. My father died and he didn't have a choice. He left me but he gave me a chance to find happiness with somebody else. It comes from trying to find the mechanism that works for you, so you get over it and it comes from having practiced it with my father. That's where it came from. It took me a long time.

I don't have too much more to say. I just wanted you to know that the child is happy.

I didn't want to speak on the child's behalf. I wanted the child to speak.

It took me three years before I could cry for my mother and during that period, all I knew was that I didn't sleep. Around the time my mum died, I was getting ready to go out. I could sense her telling me that when I came to see her, I shouldn't forget to take her something. What was I supposed to take with me? "When you come, don't forget to buy me that thing", is all I kept hearing. What was it that I was supposed to remember?

I was looking in the mirror putting rollers in my hair, then it came to me. A grey wig.

She'd had chemotherapy and had lost her hair. My mother had long, grey hair. Everybody knew her as the 'grey-haired woman'. She was grey from the age of 40. So, when she lost her hair, I bought her a grey wig. A short one. So, I was thinking *What does this mean?* I called the woman who looked after her

Chapter 15. Rachel's Story

as she was at the house at the time. I asked her if she knew where my mother's wig was. She said the last time she went to the hospital someone stole it. She didn't come back with it. When they brought her things back it wasn't there. She asked me why I wanted to know, and I smiled. My mother, excuse the pun, wouldn't have been caught dead wearing a black wig!

When I was going through the divorce, I didn't sleep much but I heard my mother's voice so many times. It would say, "You know what treat this like a transaction. Think of your children first. Put the sadness aside. Make sure you get what is yours for the sake of your children. You can't afford to be crying and getting upset, throwing things and trying to kill him. That won't get you anywhere. Think of the children."

I always feel her around me. I won't lie to you. Recently I bumped into someone and he looked at me and said, "Who is that grey-haired woman? She's always around you? I asked him what he meant. He said she was always around me and that I was a very lucky woman. I said, "I know. Thank you." He smiled and walked away.

So, when you have all this going on you don't have time for nonsense. I offend you, I say sorry and move on. I make peace. I don't want to use any of my energy to explain. Whatever emotion you feel it can't be destructive.

Chapter 16

Anne's Story

My name is Anne. I'm 59 years old. I lost my husband on April 17 of this year. We were together, oh my goodness, over 38 years. I have actually known him since I was 16. We met at a bowling alley. I used to bowl with my family. He bowled with his family. He was married at the time.

When they got separated, him and I started seeing each other and the rest is history. He had one child from his first marriage. We had a son. He's thirty-five now and our daughter is thirty-two. So, this whole journey has just been crazy.

It's totally ripped us apart. He had just turned 70 last October. The day he died was the day after my birthday. He was actually diagnosed with dementia when he was 60 so it's been quite a journey. He had a lot of health issues. And while the kids could understand, they didn't understand, because Tony always bounced back. He was put in a hospice in September of 2017. They had only given him three to six months to live but he did make it more. I attribute that to the fact that we had sold the house and moved in with our daughter and her boyfriend who had a little boy at the time. Little Tony had a lot to do with his granddad staying alive. Plus, she got pregnant again and had the baby six weeks before he died. It was a little girl. Aiden Tony, because his name was Tony. He also had one more grandson named after him – Phillip Tony. Our son was named after him. I always teased him. Why was he so special?

But moving in was a blessing and a curse because they promised to help. Really, nobody helped with anything. Nobody wanted to believe that he was actually going to die. We did have a hospice for the 18 months which was great. You know, it just gets more challenging at the end. Plus, I think my kids were still reeling. My father had gotten sick and he had passed away in December of that year.

The next year, I was diagnosed with congestive heart failure. I had to stop working which was a blessing because I was able to take care of Ray. We had moved in with my father and then I also took care of him when he was dying. We stayed there. We took care of my stepmother when she was ill. She was also in a hospice and died.

In 2016, my brother died. I had my heart surgery in 2016 too and everything with Tony just hit the fan in 2017. So, I think it's just been a multitude of shocks. Right now, my kids are not speaking with me. It's more avoidance. My daughter's words are actually she doesn't understand why I'm sad. He's not gone. He's still here.

I've started to move out of the house. I'm staying with a friend which is helping me, but I miss my grandkids. It's just affected everybody.

You know, for him and me, there's no doubt a cultural difference. He was eleven and a half years older than I was. He was married with a child. He's a Filipino. My family didn't

Chapter 16. Anne's Story

want to accept him. And his family didn't want to accept me for a while but for three years we did have it okay.

But then, of course, when he got sick at 60, all the shit just hit the fan and his family avoided him. They didn't want to deal with him. He was hard of hearing also and my daughter always told me that everybody said it just wasn't worth the effort and that really upset me. I must admit our two children were good at that point, but his family totally, totally avoided him, even quit inviting him to anything. And in all honesty, they didn't even know where we were living. When we moved into my dad's house, and he was placed in a hospice, they actually had to ask for the address to come and see him.

He was the second to the last of seven siblings and one brother is all that's left now.

The last time this brother came to see Tony was when he was diagnosed and we had come home from the hospital. I allowed the brother to come over because I was doing it for my husband, nobody else, so that my husband would be full circle when he died. In the last nine months of his life his brother didn't even bother to call, to message, to text. Nothing! But he played the crying fool when his brother died. It took years but we had a good relationship with his ex-wife which was fine. I did allow her to come and visit him though. She would come and she has a relationship with his family which is fine. She was there too just before he died with his daughter and his niece. I allowed everybody to have private time with him. And after they left, two hours later, he died in my arms.

As for money, you know, there's not much. Nobody offered to help with anything during the illness and of course, things cost. So, what I had gotten as an inheritance from my father was probably all spent on him. There is nothing for the kids because I used the money on his services and caregiving and so on and so forth.

I feel my kids are relieved, honestly, that he's gone but I also think they feel the wrong parent has died. My daughter would always tell me she would have put him in a nursing home at the end. He was catheterised due to trauma from the tube, his penis was splitting so he wasn't able to wear the pull-ups or anything – not that you could see anything with the way his shirts were – but she always told me that I should be putting him in a nursing home. And I know if I would have been the one to go first, they would have put their dad in a nursing home and just ignored him. Right now, they're totally ignoring me and avoiding me. There's not even a phone call, a "Hi, how are you?" It's sad. I've been trying to catch up with my health and not once have either one of my kids said, "Hey, how's the doctor's appointments going?" And they know I'm going to the doctors.

Grief? Forget it! Apparently, they don't believe in grief because they keep telling me I'm young, I should be travelling, I should go on trips. I should be meeting somebody. Really? He's only been gone five months. This is the man that I had been with for 39 years and it's crazy.

I miss him. I don't want anybody. Nobody's going to replace him. That part – I don't even want to go there, because it's incomprehensible. The way I'm grieving, they don't understand because I'm not letting them see me. They're assuming something that's totally different.

I'm trying to cope with these doctor's appointments. I don't even want to do it and I have two friends of mine that are forcing me to do it. But my kids think that I'm just lying

Chapter 16. Anne's Story

around crying, doing nothing. I'm trying to cope. It's hard to cope. So, they honestly have no idea. Their way of coping is you cannot talk about him, you cannot bring him up.

I showed Little Tony a picture of him sitting on his Papa's lap. My daughter got very upset thinking I was showing Papa, which I wasn't. I was just trying to show him how much his little sister looks like him and I totally got reamed out for it. It seems like even when I'm playing with the kids, it's an inconvenience, a burden, that I'm interfering, which is one of the reasons I'm in the process of leaving the house. My daughter has actually said to me – because I told her that his family has never reached out since the service, "Well, they're sad so you should be reaching out to them." I don't think so! I'm the one who did the sleepless nights. I am the one who didn't sleep for days on end, didn't eat, didn't have any life, went to the doctor's, hardly saw friends. They never came to see him. Call. Reach out. I will have nothing to do with that side of his family anymore. As far as I'm concerned, I may carry his last name but that does not obligate me to his family.

My daughter has been outspoken about the fact that even though he's gone, I will, according to her, still acknowledge the two children, the grandchildren from his daughter, my stepdaughter, and she will make sure that I provide gifts and so forth. And I find that pretty funny that she will advocate for everybody else – his brother, her uncle, his daughter, her sister, the grandchildren, so on and so forth but she doesn't advocate for me. The day after his service a niece came from Canada and all of them got together for breakfast. My daughter went. I was not invited. I was not included. Nobody advocated for me. What I had done, I honestly can't answer that.

But nobody, nobody over this whole journey of him being ill ever thought of him. I know their friends have seen it. It's been confirmed to me. Nobody can understand that. I'm allowed to feel sad. I do feel sad. I'm not breaking down in public. I'm not throwing fits. I do break up and I try to choke it back. My tears are private for me or with my friends that I know I can trust and that haven't deserted me.

I feel that my children honestly do feel that I should have been the first one to die because they could have gotten him into a nursing home, and he would have died very shortly without me. They're excluding me from anything and everything in their lives. And they're only dealing with his side of the family. I have nobody left on my side. My parents, my brother, everybody's gone. So, my children and grandchildren are the only ones that I do have left.

You know, it's just a horrible thing. They watched him decline. They saw this man go from 220 pounds to 130 pounds. With the dementia, he basically died from malnutrition. He was a shell of what he was. But the day he died, he told me that morning that he loved me. Those were his last words.

I always tried to keep those kids up-to-date on everything. I did text chains to all three of them and then everybody just became so disinterested because it was taking daddy so long to die. It just tears everybody apart. So, there's no money that's going to benefit them. They're actually worried about my life insurance policy and who's going to get that and it's not much. I've made sure my arrangements are taken care of including seven blood grandchildren to think of, so they can fight when I'm done.

Chapter 16. Anne's Story

The sad part is there's no uniformity in this. There's no compassion. There's no thoughtfulness to me as a mother, as their mother, as his wife, as their children's grandmother. My eldest granddaughter from my son, she's eight. And my son's wife and I did not have a very good relationship. She's a very distant person. And the eight-year-old told me after my husband died, that it was a shame that mommy and daddy never invited Papa and Nima, that's what we're called, to their birthday parties. And she's told me how she told her dad, shame on him now that Papa was gone, they need to invite Nima. Yet my son and my daughter-in-law didn't even tell the grandchildren, their children, the remaining four of them. Only the eldest one. They did not bring the children to the service, except for the 15-year-old which I understand.

But my daughter-in-law didn't want us around the house when they're having parties.

And I got it. She doesn't like me. She was okay with Tony but at least do it for your dad, due to the fact she knew he was dying. She came up to me at his service and she gave me this big hug. Never said a word and to me that was so phoney.

They finally, finally invited me to a birthday party in June. I did go for two of the grandchildren. She ignored me completely. So, I can't even understand why the heck you're gonna hug me because it's phoney and I won't deal with the phoniness.

Ten years ago, I had even said when he died I would do a private service and to hell with his family, his brother, the in-laws, his ex, his daughter, everybody, except for my children. I would do a private service because I didn't feel anybody needed to be around him. If you weren't around him when he was living do not come and grieve over him when he's dead. If you didn't come and see him when he could hear you, when he could acknowledge you, when he could love you, I don't need you over his coffin.

I gave in to everything for people to be around him. Just due to the fact it was full circle for him. I made sure that everything was done right. We're Catholic and were brought up in the Philippines. I made sure he had the last rites. Everything was done properly. I gave him the service that he wanted. I let those people in. I included his ex-wife in his obituary. I did it for him not for me! I honestly do certain things sometimes. Did I do wrong? But it wasn't about me, it was about him. And I can't change the past anyway. I just don't know why people cannot understand.

You watch somebody just deteriorate before your eyes. You know, just being confused, not eating, not drinking, not remembering things, struggling to walk, struggling to do any bodily functions. How many times this poor man fell, how much assistance he needed, and so few people offered to assist. Even living with our daughter, there was very little assistance. I know it was more of an intrusion but it was good for me to move in there with him because I was paying the rent and I did give her money when we first moved in.

But those discussions I wasn't having, because my husband was the priority. I don't know...money is totally the root of all evil. I know my son was pissed but when my dad died, he walked away with a lot of money that he was supposed to just distribute to my daughter and I and he didn't. So, when everything was said and done with my husband, I took care of him. I did what I had to do to make sure we weren't

Chapter 16. Anne's Story

burdening my daughter financially. But I guess we burdened them emotionally just being in the house.

So, the whole bottom line of this is there's no support. People disappear. He had a good friend, Gerry, who used to call me at least every two weeks. When things were getting bad and we knew Tony was not gonna last much longer, he was calling me every day sometimes two times a day. It's now been four months since I've heard from him. I was friends with his wife. I haven't heard from her since the service. People have just gone and hidden in the woodwork. I know people don't like to deal with somebody who's sad. I try to hold my emotions in check when I am around somebody because I try not to make other people uncomfortable.

When it comes to this, other people should not be my priority. I'm not asking anybody to talk about him. I'm not asking anybody to be there for me to do things for me. But it just seems like since he's taken his last breath, everybody has disappeared. Totally. And out of my family, my son's eldest boy, who's 15, is the one I talk and text. He's like mine and Tony's baby. The other kids are all smaller. I haven't heard from my stepdaughter, haven't heard from his brother. Haven't heard from anybody and that's fine. That part of my life is a closed chapter. My son who used to call me every day, up to three times a day, no longer does.

My daughter. It's very uncomfortable. I know we need to have a discussion. I don't know who's going to be ready to start this. She can't understand what I'm doing. She actually told me I've gone bat shit crazy and broke. Maybe I have, but I'm trying to survive. I think I have the right to feel sad for him. I miss him! What a do over. It tears me up. I've got part of his ashes in my purse. He goes everywhere with me. People assume, people judge.

Honestly, I feel that he wasn't worth the money to them so it's not even worth their grief or their tears. They're treating me as if I don't exist, like life would be better off without me. Right now, I'm using avoidance…it's how I'm coping. It's a sad life but I'd do it all over again, that's the stupidest part. My daughter's friend asked me, had I known back in the day, what was going to be if I would still marry him. I would marry him a billion plus times over.

People don't understand that I miss the cup of coffee in the morning, the conversations we used to have. I miss talking to him. It's lonely. I just know our family is not a family anymore. I always told my kids that I fought for my family and my marriage but I found out the hard way that I obviously don't have those paths and that's sad.

But you know, I'm really glad, honestly, now that I know all this, that I've lived all this. I am glad he did go first. Don't take that the wrong way because if I'd gone first, they would have neglected him. They would have put him away. He would have died alone. They've shown me the kind of treatment that he would have gotten if I wasn't here. Nobody was ever going to take care of him. That's just wrong. What's that saying? Parents can take care of ten children, but ten children can't take care of their parents. How true it is.

I always tried to make sure on Father's Day, his birthday, the kids had to be around to acknowledge him. I'm 59 and I have not seen my son since my 50th birthday. Not even on Mother's Day since then. And that's fine. You can ignore me, but I refuse to have my husband ignored.

Chapter 16. Anne's Story

And now this death. It's just cemented that obviously we're not a family and the longer the time is going on we're not going to be a family. I can just feel myself pulling further and further away. And I know they are too and I know my daughter is just as stubborn as I am. My son will do anything the wife says. She leads him around.

So, money or no money, we're all apart. Grief or no grief, we're all apart. They don't care. They honestly cannot care. When you can't even get a text message that says, "Hi, how are you?" And believe me, I've reached out. I've called them all. I've asked them how the kids are, if the kids are sick and I get one word answers. You can only reach out so far.

My husband's death has just been a total explosion. The man who always protected was no longer there. He had even asked my daughter three weeks before he died to take care of mommy. She stood there telling him mommy's gonna live with us, and I'm not holding her to deathbed promises because you don't stay where you don't belong.

I mean nothing! My dad's death was hard to get through because my kids had issues with it, but we came around from that. I don't see us coming around from Tony and it'll never happen with his family. And that's fine. I was just as complete when they didn't talk to him or me and I'm fine with that. But my grandkids, that's sad that I'm losing that from my husband's death. I've got a six-month-old grandchild that I'm not even getting to know. Is this life going to get any better? God only knows. You go to sleep at night and just pray to God you don't wake up. I know there's a purpose, but I just don't get it anymore. I can't do this anymore.

I'm done! Done!

Chapter 17

Penelope's Story

My name is Penelope. I am a 56-year-old wife and mother of three wonderful children, my beautiful gifts from God. Nearly 11 years ago my life was completely turned upside down and I didn't think I would live to tell this story. Up until then, I had mostly led a happy life, because of my usually happy nature and God's abundant blessings. Then, in 2008, my beloved husband Phillip died.

I met my husband in London in 1988 and it was one of those special relationships where you feel like you've known the person all your life. Three months into dating and he was already talking about marriage. Even before we got married in 1989 and had our children, he had become my best friend. We settled into our busy lives in London both working and caring for our young family. I remember pinching myself and wondering how I could be so lucky with a handsome, intelligent, well-built, honest and very loving man. We couldn't go a day without calling each other despite our pressured jobs.

Financially I was so secure. I never discussed finances with anybody because I was acutely aware that I was very blessed in that area too. Phillip was so generous and would do anything for the kids and me. He paid for everything in the house, all our holidays and lots of gifts. Even outside of Christmas, birthdays and anniversaries, he would often give me his card to go shopping. Apart from work, we were rarely apart, simply because we enjoyed each other's company so much. Nine days before he died, on my 46th birthday, Phillip surprised me with a carefully planned party after taking me to Warwickshire for the day.

Monday morning, 10 November 2008, was the worst day of my life. That day, in the early hours, my fit and healthy husband suffered a fatal heart attack in his sleep and was pronounced dead an hour after arriving at the hospital. To say I was in shock and totally devastated is an understatement. I will never forget the mix of emotions that morning, the most dominant being complete shock, sadness and fear. I also immediately felt alone and a need to protect myself and my children although I couldn't work out who I wanted to protect us from. I remember on the drive back from the hospital, I saw mothers walking their kids to school. I saw people hurriedly walking to catch their trains or buses and I remember thinking everything in the world seemed normal while my life was over.

From that moment, I was surrounded by love. God sent me my family and some very precious friends who dropped everything on that Monday morning to be with me. By 11 o'clock (Phillip died at 4 o'clock) there were 35 people in our home, all like me, in a state of total shock as they had all seen Phillip the week before at my surprise party. Some would turn my home into their office and work from there. Friends arranged a rota system to ensure there would be at

Chapter 17. Penelope's Story

least one person staying with us every night. Food, drinks, money, human presence, messages came flooding in.

My mother immediately left Ghana and arrived in London the next day with my dad following three days later. My siblings arrived from their various bases to support me, with one of them living and working from my home so he could be around the children and me. I had people around me 24/7 and yet I was remarkably lonely.

Sleep was non-existent. I hadn't realised how very long nights were until then. I would doze off for 30 minutes then wake up thinking I'd had a nightmare. I had lost my best friend, husband, lover, father of my children, the person who made us laugh, who brought music to our home, who was the life and soul of the party, who was very honest, a sharp dresser, intelligent doctor, the unique and extraordinary Phillip who I was fortunate to call my husband. Financially, 60% of our household income went that day.

Whilst my family and friends rallied around me, my in-laws turned against me. Rather than uniting with me to give him a befitting burial, they started disagreements which ended in the total separation of our two families. We did not speak again from 2009 to 2018. Disagreements ranged from where to bury him to who had been left out of writing a tribute – such trivial matters in the face of a huge loss. I had really tried to engage them at every step of the funeral planning process. They had forgotten that there were three children, aged 19, 15 and nine, who had lost their rock and their hero and if us adults did not understand what had happened, imagine what the children felt!

Phillip was the last of nine children, and at no point did any of his siblings ask how I was going to cope with looking after the children. There was no burning desire to stop focusing on totally irrelevant matters when there were more important matters such as the welfare of the children. In the end, on the first anniversary, they demanded to know what had been left to them. It was most disappointing because I thought I had a good relationship with them. They knew I needed every penny to look after my kids. So, to ask me for a share of what Phillip had left was cruel. And now my children have grown up without the support of that half of their family. Whilst we have made a little progress in reconciling, a lot of damage has been done which will take time to undo.

I must say at this point that not all my in-laws took a stance against me. Some of them gave me their full support and have been in constant touch with me to this day. At the same time, to date, more than ten years on, there are in-laws who have never called me. Fortunately, the good people far outweigh the bad and the saying 'a friend in need is a friend indeed' is so true in times like this.

Of all the many friends and family who supported me in various ways when my husband died, I found the most comfort in letters I received from those who had been through it themselves. I realised I wasn't alone, and I was comforted by the fact that months and years on, they had all lived to tell the tale; they could at last speak about their loved ones and smile without the pain and sorrow of the early months. I also found great comfort from people who I didn't know but who took the time and effort to write or even phone me. It told me that the world is still full of love and people who really care.

I concluded that in this grieving process, you are alone. Everyone in the society we come from professes to know what you ought to do to whilst grieving: wear black all year, don't go out, don't date, remain in a room without coming out for a week, bury him this way or that. Losing my husband felt like being in a furnace all the time and, every now and then, you find a cool spot (an oasis in a desert) where you want to remain forever. Unfortunately, you go straight back into the furnace after a short enjoyable stay in that cool spot. That cool spot is different for everybody and no one can determine yours for you. It may be retail therapy, it may be being alone, it may be being with friends; it is anything that makes you happy even for five minutes. I found my cool spot was when I was with friends and family and my goodness, my friends and family were excellent.

In the beginning I didn't believe it when I was told that God would see me through and comfort my children and me. My Christian faith was shaken but I realise now that God is great and ever-loving…all the time. He never promised us a life free of problems. He promised to be there for us in times of turmoil and He has been there for my children and me. I took baby steps towards healing – taking each day as it came, looking forward to the next day, week, month, season or milestones. The anniversaries in the first year were hard. I felt like I couldn't breathe sometimes and every now and then I was able to come up for air. I had to decide to swim or sink. My children have been a great source of strength to me. Not wanting them to suffer more than they already had, I resolved to be strong for them and to carry on with all the plans my husband and I had for them. So, whilst he was physically absent, I had to make the house run as though he was still around. I took on contracting jobs to make up for the loss in income and keep the kids in the life they were accustomed to and that was hard. I say this in the full knowledge that not everyone is fortunate enough to be able to fill the financial void when they lose a husband and I thank God every day for always meeting me at the point of my need, for never leaving us nor forsaking us, and for being a Father to the fatherless as He promised in the Bible.

It's really hard to manage your own grief plus your young children's grief plus working hard to cope financially, plus have this gaping big hole in your life. On top of all that you have to deal with lack of respect or care from people including some of your own friends and family. If only members of our community knew the extra pressures they put on widows with the imposition of rules and the placing of unnecessary demands, all in the name of culture and what this can do to a widow's health and well-being. I came to the realisation that many widows in Ghana have been subjected to cruelty from in-laws and other family on top of the loss of income, loss of their home or other properties, loss of their livelihood, happiness and joy plus the loneliness and the absence after the physical and spiritual closeness of their spouse. My own paternal grandmother went through this in 1950 when my granddad died. My dad was 17 and a student at Achimota School. My grandmother then died very early, possibly due to the stresses of losing her husband and income and later her home, which was taken by relatives.

I remember hiding my grief because I was worried that people would stop visiting if I cried all the time. And I remember how disturbed and extremely sad my children became when they saw me crying. So, I tried hard not to cry in their presence. I put a lot of pressure on myself to feel better quickly and gave myself unrealistic timelines by when I should have moved on and be done with grieving. In our society, the statement 'damned if you do and damned if you don't' rings true in all aspects of our lives, but never truer than when you lose a loved one. Everybody in Ghana had their own opinions on what you did, didn't do or should have done. I was accused of stressing my husband and therefore causing his heart attack. I was also accused of stealing all his possessions – possessions he and I had built together after we came to the UK with nothing.

My story took a different turn when I was contacted by my ex-boyfriend. I met him at university in 1982 and we dated for five years. We broke up in London in 1988, post-university, and went our separate ways. I had not seen him for twenty-two years and he had married and divorced in that time. When we started communicating in 2010, it was one of the best things that happened in my recovery. When I couldn't sleep, he would call me and we would talk for hours. We got married in 2013 and even though it was not plain sailing at the start because change is hard and because we underestimate grief sometimes in our haste to move on and fill the void, I am happy to have a lovely gentleman to share my life with once again. We have undertaken this adventure at an older and more mature age, and it feels so good to have him in my life again. I thank God. Even with this second phase, Ghanaians had a lot to say: "She's marrying too soon", "She couldn't have loved her husband," "She might have been having an affair with him while she was married," "He must be looking for something from her." The list went on and on.

None of us will live forever but for reasons known to God alone, some are called much too soon. We never get over the loss of a loved one; we learn to live with it and accept it. At the start of the grieving process, our time in the cool spot is brief and the cool spots are few and far between. As the years go by, the time in the cool spot gets longer and longer. It does not mean we do not fall into the furnace every now and then but it's comforting to know the heat is less intense and less time is spent there than at the start.

Chapter 18

To Whom It May Concern

Afi

Afi's story broke my heart; not just because of the loss of her husband but also because she was a young woman, only 27, who had to go through such a bitter experience. I remember when I was that age – young, inexperienced and unsure of my own voice and identity. How would I have pulled myself out of such an experience? I'm over 20 years older than Afi and I know how hard it's been without the support and knowledge of how to deal with grief in a way that works for you. Culturally, as Ghanaians, we don't do confrontation and any attempt to address issues full-on will most certainly get you a reputation.

I recall speaking with Afi and telling her how I didn't want my face to be seen at the funeral as I found it excruciating to have my grief on display. Her response surprised me.

"You couldn't have done that if you were in Ghana. You would have to show your face."

I couldn't imagine having to be forced to do anything on the day of my husband's burial that I didn't want to do. It led us to speak about how she was treated and why having a voice is so vital.

Afi was bewildered and in shock when she lost her young husband as would be expected. Nothing could have prepared her for what ensued. The denial of her unborn child is something she struggled with but shamefully, it is very common when a woman loses her husband and is 'cursed' with being pregnant. You're immediately relegated from wife to scarlet woman. No evidence of infidelity is required, and you are blamed some way, somehow, for the loss of your husband.

I cannot fathom what Afi went through and what her experience has done to her life. To still be reliant on medication and mental health support is an indication of the depths of her trauma, compounded by having to keep this a secret from her nearest and dearest.

Removing her children from her is another trauma she was subjected to. In terms of her grieving process, this was probably one of the worst things that could have happened. That was another loss – the boys remaining with her would have been a source of comfort and strength and a reason to live and get better. Taking them away placed her in a position of loss of value and an uninterrupted space of having to dwell on the loss of her husband. They would have been a welcome distraction from her pain.

The impact of loss on our mental health is profound. Having explained the various processes of grief that takes hold, it's imperative that the treatment of the bereaved person is saturated in gentleness, compassion, love and patience. The moment you're made to feel like as if you are in a war zone, depending on your character, can cause untold psychological damage.

When I listened to Afi's story, what hit me was the intensity of her grief. It was hard to believe it had not been a recent bereavement and I wondered in those moments if she ever would have a part of her heart healed. Everything that she could seemingly have used to try to comfort herself was ripped away – her integrity being called into question as a wife, the ability to raise her own children and, sadly, the memories of her husband through keepsakes of their life together being disposed of. I cannot see Afi in any of the processes here; she is told what to do because culture or tradition demands it, with nothing but silence from all parties within supporting what could have sent her to an early grave.

Traditions are man-made, some are good, and some don't serve us well. Tradition has an important role to play across all communities but the moment it makes a victim out of someone, we must be willing at the very least to challenge or question it. What happened to Afi shouldn't ever be allowed to happen again. She isn't the only person to suffer. Considering she had a son old enough to know that he had lost his daddy isn't something to be overlooked.

I attended an amazing conference with a world-renowned paediatrician, Dr Nadine Burke Harris, who is known for her work on Adverse Childhood Experiences (ACEs). Dr Burke Harris explains how untreated childhood trauma can lead to several health issues in adulthood, including certain cancers. Her work is vast and cannot be discussed in extensive detail here but there is one overarching theme. If a child faces abuse, separation from a parent, bereavement, being brought up in a home where there is domestic violence, neglect or bullying (to name a few), these experiences can have an adverse effect on the child. When trauma goes untreated, it can expose a child to a plethora of health issues both physical and mental in adulthood.

In general, we don't give children enough consideration when they have been bereaved. We don't always allow them to speak of their loss. Silence for anyone that wants to speak about their loss is a killer in itself. The level of damage this can do is untold, yet it's ironic that even within my culture, the widow isn't allowed to speak. What resonated with me, listening to Afi's story, is how much we need to be aware of how our actions can impact not only the widow but also her children. We must care enough to change behaviours to minimise the devastation they are already feeling.

Penelope

The start of Penelope's issues was the squabbling within the family over where her husband was to be buried. In her culture, the body of the person who has passed away belongs to the family and not solely to the spouse, so things aren't as cut and dried in terms of doing what one pleases – if you are to adhere to tradition that is.

There is little or no consideration about how distressing this aspect of the process is. Too often, demands are made without considering the human element. It's all well and good talking tradition and culture, but what about the people involved? Is it too much to fathom how much this is affecting them? After all, it's the wife and children who lived with the

Chapter 18. To Whom It May Concern

person who has passed away, day in and day out; so, imagine how the children must have felt, one minute having their father there before bedtime but gone by the next morning? Who considers the impact on those immediately affected with reminders all around their home of what they have lost? Would it be unreasonable to expect the wife and children to want to be near their husband and father to lay flowers, to visit and to know that he is near instead of being buried miles away? Tradition and culture most certainly have their place, but consideration of people's feelings and needs should always be a priority, whatever the circumstance.

Penelope's need to protect herself and her children, but not knowing from what, was interesting. Unfortunately, like many of us, there was indeed a need for protection and self-preservation. The inability of her in-laws to unite and support her and the children led to a separation over many, many years. When you are in this situation of isolation or alienation from people that you may have been quite close to is sad. You may even blame yourself, but don't. You can only control your behaviour, never that of others. When you have real friends and people who love you and want to support you, you really can't put a price on that. It feeds your soul. It gives you the strength you need to face the day and enables you to experience a certain level of normalcy because you know you're supported.

Inheritance is a huge thing in any culture but, in West Africa, we seem to have it down to a fine art. We can often be so brazen about it. How do you allow yourself to be so absent at the most crucial time of one's suffering but happy to reappear to ask for what may or may not have been left for you? It's almost as if it's what's left behind that is of value and importance, as opposed to the life that was loved and lost way too soon. It is not unusual for families to forget they are family once money is involved. The loss, now that money or property is available, pales into insignificance because greed rears its ugly head. Most definitely people grieve differently but rarely do you have a whole personality transplant. Greed should never be confused with grief and sometimes people choose to use the guise of grief to perpetuate the most appalling of behaviours.

Penelope's experience with grief and subsequent remarriage taught me that a new husband doesn't simply replace the old. The grieving never ends and the celebration of that life never stops. The shock of a sudden death is horrible, but I feel it's further compounded when you have a beautiful marriage and really shared your life with your soulmate. How can such a happy and beautiful life be shattered like that. It's hard not to be dramatic and think it's one big conspiracy against you. What else can one say? It just doesn't make sense how or why this would happen. A beautiful marriage, three wonderful children, great careers, a lovely home and you go to bed like any other night. But it's not like any other night; your life is about to change beyond all recognition within hours. How do you pull yourself out of such a life-changing event and all the additional troubles it brings to be in a place where you can even consider going into another relationship?

From the way Penelope describes her marriage, it was beautiful and complete. She not only lost her husband but also her friend, her lover and her companion. The truth about losing a husband is that you lose so many things when they die. You lose the one person you can tell a secret to and know it goes no further and the only person you share your bed with. You learn to be intimate in a way that you rarely are with others that goes beyond the physical – and then it's gone.

When you have this kind of a marriage, the bar can be set so high that you may feel that nobody else could possibly meet up to that expectation. Nobody else could possibly love you like that, or you them. But is that always the case or do we not give ourselves the chance to have that again? Is that how we feel or is it that we are too afraid of what people will say? I remember visiting my Indian dentist with my daughter for our yearly check-up. I told her the devastating news of losing my husband and she immediately asked how my daughter was holding up as she had also lost her father when she was 12 years old. She proceeded to tell me how difficult it was for her, but I felt encouraged that she was a dentist, now married herself, so I know there's hope for my own child in terms of living a full life. The next question I asked was how her mother had coped and if she had remarried, especially as she had mentioned her mother was in her 30s when she had been widowed.

"Oh no, she couldn't do that!" she said with indignation. "Our community wouldn't allow it!"

I can't recall what I said in response to that revelation, but I knew how unfair I thought it was. Had it been her choice not to remarry, that would have been fine, but to have that imposed on her seemed so harsh. To sentence someone to a life of loneliness and to have to be responsible for her children with no prospect of having a husband to help her was unjust in my mind.

Penelope was very nearly relegated to the perpetual state of widow if she hadn't been strong enough to follow her own heart and mind. To be told it was 'too soon' to remarry after five years is excessive to say the least, especially for the reasons she was asked to wait. We often fear the judgement and condemnation of others, but the truth is, like all news, people will move on to what they perceive to be the next hot topic. Why deprive yourself of living your best life because of what others might say? Absolutely, it's easier said than done but it comes down to one thing at the end of the day – do you want to be happy or do you want to wear a mask for the rest of your life, pretending to be content with your lot? Are you going to resign yourself to a life of celibacy or are you going to be having relationships behind closed doors to avoid wagging tongues? It's certainly not an enviable position to be in but Penelope made the right decision for herself by marrying her knight in shining armour with the blessing of her children and I think in that, there's a good lesson. Seek the approval or support, for want of a better word, from those who have not only your best interests at heart, but also those who will advise and support you from a place of emotional and societal independence; anything else may be another form of control.

Penelope's story is encouraging and should be a source of hope for those who are widowed and don't believe they can ever love again.

Rachel

Rachel found it difficult at first to speak about her experience of bereavement. She said something quite profound when we spoke. She said she didn't want to tell her story as

Chapter 18. To Whom It May Concern

a grown woman. Rachel told me that she had never given the child a chance to speak, and she wanted to sit with me to tell someone what it felt like being her at a tender age, losing both her parents.

I was so humbled and filled with sadness and compassion by her words because it made me think of my own daughter and whether her voice had been heard enough.

I let Rachel speak and was alarmed to hear of three major bereavements in her short life at the time – each one reinforcing the feelings of invisibility, guilt and responsibility and a burden no child should carry. It was sad to hear that all it would have taken was a reassuring word from a loving adult to put to rest these destructive feelings of guilt for both her and her brother. Yet that never came. Then on top of that, her brother was also burdened by an expectation of responsibility he thought he had to meet because of traditional and cultural norms.

Rachel's take on how she was being treated as a child has shaped how she communicates with and has raised her own children – with complete transparency. Her assessment of her emotional and mental ability to understand all that was going on around her is something adults can use to learn about children. It's like warring parents in the same home, trying to act normally and keep the issues away from the kids. The truth is this rarely works because children can pick things up from the atmosphere or spirit in the home and know that something is amiss, no matter how well we try to smile and act as if all is well. What Rachel is saying is that children know.

Can we be more open with our children and create a safe space for them to be themselves and truly say what's on their young minds, so we can help them in their journeys too? It seems we leave them even less tended to than the adults and this is quite dangerous, considering the limiting beliefs, self-condemnation and confusion that they go through and grow up with. Guilt in the grieving process has got to be for me, one of the biggest hindrances to healing. The process of healing is exactly that – a process with no definitive end and to add guilt puts an unnecessary hurdle in the way. Guilt and a child should never be placed in the same space but if it happens, we must have open dialogue with them; this dialogue should gently steer them to a safe place in their heads where they can process their pain without being further burdened.

Rachel's take on the treatment of her mentally ill mother caused her to be protective of her mother at the expense of what she really wanted for herself. She wanted to go to a particular school but felt compelled to look after her mother. Support was lacking even in that decision she made. It is essential we try to consciously support children who are bereaved. In Rachel's case, she faced this fate three times. The adults around her didn't have her best interests at heart because the murmurings, judgement and expectations placed on a sick mother by relatives; this meant she had no safe adult to go to for reassurance or encouragement, so continue to perform the position she had taken on as caregiver. Rachel's take on the treatment of her mentally ill mother made her protective of her mother at the expense of what she really wanted for herself. She wanted to go to a particular school but abandoned that idea as she was compelled to look after her mother. Support was lacking when she had to make that decision. It is essential we try to consciously support children who are bereaved. In Rachel's case, she faced this fate three times. The adults

Chapter 18. To Whom It May Concern

around her didn't have her best interests at heart because of the murmurings, judgement and expectations placed on a sick mother by relatives; this meant she had no adult to go to for reassurance or encouragement. All she could do was continue in her role as caregiver.

There are many children that care for a sick relative and we must never underestimate how difficult this task is. Look at how difficult it is for adults. It's a job that isn't for the faint-hearted as it's emotionally, mentally and sometimes physically taxing; we must care enough to help ease the burden in any way we can. I don't think Rachel expected help and that is the sad part. After all, most of the adults that had made huge declarations of assistance about their welfare never quite materialised. The betrayal and isolation must have been a real disappoint for her and she just had to keep things ticking for herself emotionally.

Rachel's mother was known to suffer from mental illness, though there wasn't a diagnosis they could use to put a name to it; but what about those who go through some form of mental illness following bereavement? The loss of a loved one has varying effects on an individual and it's clear that some people cope better than others, depending on a lot of factors, from personality, relationship to the person they have lost and the support they receive, to name a few.

What about those who develop a mental illness following bereavement? The loss of a loved one has varying effects on an individual and it's clear that some people cope better than others for a variety of reasons both intrinsic and extrinsic. Falling into depression isn't unusual and how deeply that depression affects someone or how long it lasts varies. I have heard many bereaved say they don't want to live, that they want to go and be with the person they have lost and some really do feel suicidal. These are some of the other reasons why it's so important to hold those who are bereaved close and gently try to the best of our ability to be the emotional support they need. People who have faced a loss don't need to be told to be strong – *we* need to be strong for them. Strength is the one thing you rarely feel when you lose someone you love. The effects of the loss can also manifest physically. There is loss of sleep, loss of appetite, heart problems and general aches and pains to name a few. I recall having to put my left wrist in a support bandage for a while. I hadn't realised I would literally sit for hours with my head resting in the palm of my hand, staring into space. The lack of movement in my wrist caused excruciating muscular pain.

Rachel speaks of insomnia that plagued her in her childhood. This was because many times she would wake to her mother having gone; sleep then symbolised her mother's disappearance to a mental institution. Insomnia still haunts her because her grieving process started before the actual physical loss of either parent. Physical symptoms of grief and loss can be real areas of concern, especially in children, because it may be hard for them to express their feelings or be able to adequately articulate them. We must try to pay attention and see where we can make a difference in easing their fear and frustration. We must be open to them getting professional help when needed.

Let's consider our behaviour, our words and actions around and towards children who are just about figuring how this big, wide world works after they lose one of the most important people in their life.

Anne

Anne's story gives us another perspective on how the grief journey is experienced by many people. She speaks of the feeling of abandonment, not only from friends, but from some of her closest family members. Her family seems to be fragmented since the loss of her husband and finding a way to navigate through that loss and manage the feuds with her children must have been particularly difficult.

Many people complain about feeling deserted following bereavement. The reasons for this range from others feeling they should have moved on, to the bereaved putting on a brave face that leads others to think they are coping better than they are. They do this perhaps because they want to avoid upsetting those around them or feeling like they are a burden to their nearest and dearest.

Falling out with family after a death somehow appears to be a necessary evil that one must experience. As much as losing a loved one can bring people closer, in too many cases it can tear the family apart. Sometimes when a strong and important figure within a family passes away, the very fabric of the home seems to disintegrate. For those left behind, the shift in the family dynamics can be profound.

Anne experienced a lot of loss and had to soldier on despite what she had gone through. She felt abandoned possibly because her children, especially her daughter, was also struggling to come to terms with the loss of her father. Her daughter had no understanding of how Anne was feeling so it was hard for Anne. She wanted to acknowledge the loss and grieve in a manner that was in line with her understanding of loss and its magnitude, but her daughter on the other hand was in a different headspace.

Because this journey is so painful and so unique to the individual, I personally don't feel it's possible to call Anne's case. Mother and daughter are both grieving in ways that are symbolic of where they are within the cycles of grief. If either party tries to impose their will on the other, in even the slightest way, they will continue to widen the wedge between them.

When someone dies, they are connected and associated with many people and many things, all with different and special meanings to those who knew and loved them. Each person is going to mourn them in their own way that helps them handle the loss. Conflict can arise if one party feels the other isn't doing it right. Time that could be spent comforting one another now becomes time spent at each other's throats or avoiding one another. I honestly feel some form of conflict resolution and a safe space created for both mother and daughter could have helped to put things in perspective and allowed for both parties to see things through the other person's emotional lens.

It's a wonder to see how divergent Anne and her children are with respect to their perspective on how far along the grief journey she is. She is being pushed out of the nest and encouraged to date five months after losing her spouse because she is still young and needs to get out there. Anne is not ready though. Yet there are other families who would have plenty to say about her dating even years after a husband's death. There would be no issue if Anne felt she was ready, but because she doesn't, time fails to place any true perspective on her situation.

Major events like marriage, the birth of children or a death can be a time where these differences are highlighted, and these are not always positive differences. After a death, there can be a tug of war over the person who has passed away, as death somehow makes people want to observe cultural and traditional demands more than usual. Anne's experience of her in-laws not wanting to support the husband emotionally is something we see frequently, and I am yet to figure out why this is the case. We seem to run for the hills at a time when our loved ones need us the most. I don't know if it's a fear of responsibility or because we feel someone else is meeting that responsibility so we don't have to. Anne put the needs of her husband first and allowed his brother to see him when he was first diagnosed; notice that though Anne probably would not have wanted to engage with her brother-in-law, she did so because she knew her husband may have wanted that. Maybe that could have been a time for her brother-in-law to offer some support and help establish a relationship that was more positive considering his brother was terminally ill.

It is very painful for those who have been there so selflessly for a loved one who passes away to watch those who deserted that person mourning above everyone else. It is hard to swallow what appears to be crocodile tears, but who really knows? Grief does strange things to people.

Looking after a sick spouse is hard. No matter how much you love your partner, shifting between being spouse, carer and advocate is no mean feat. It's very sad to witness your once-vibrant and larger-than-life spouse withering away. The emotional, mental and physical pressure you are under is immense and it's a time where many people are left feeling isolated and overwhelmed.

Of course, when someone is ill, the focus is very much on them as that is who has the immediate need and who is ultimately suffering. However, very often the carer is forgotten. Seldom do they complain or indeed ask for any help so it's easy to forget how tough the physical investment in taking care of a sick person is. When the illness is terminal, imagine how heartbreaking it is for the carer to witness that all their best efforts appear to have come to nothing. It's a particularly sensitive and stressful time for them and Anne was no different. When you are putting in such unconditional love in supporting a sick spouse, it can be very hurtful and discouraging to get no moral support from the family of the person who is ill.

People take it for granted that their spouse will automatically take care of them during an illness but that isn't always the case. Some people for various reasons can't handle it, and I could not possibly judge them. For those that stay, we should do our best to encourage, support, relieve and ease the stress of such a huge responsibility occasionally. A phone call, a visit or a cooked meal can break the routine and be an enormous morale boost for all involved.

I cannot stress enough, especially listening to the tearful account of Anne, how much a little concern and compassion could have helped her cope with the loss of someone she'd loved for 39 years. The loneliness following such a loss is indescribable, especially when you had a solid and close union.

Sadly, sometimes we don't have a lot to hold on to other than the immense love and service to the one we promised to cherish in sickness and in health. We hope this sacrifice is enough to help block out the pain of isolation and desertion and create a haven of sorts in our minds to counter voices and reminders of the pain we are left with.

Chapter 19

A Penny for Your Thoughts

I think by now it's fair to say, death is a tough subject to tackle. It would also be fair to say it's harder to talk about death and financial provision, or the lack thereof for some more than others.

Africans are, in general, a very religious people who practise traditional religions, Christianity or Islam. Recognising and worshipping a higher power is very much a way of life and it's deemed strange or unusual for someone of African descent not to be practising some sort of religion. It would be reasonable therefore to conclude that religion plays such a huge part within the community that the standards set in it are generally used as a guide for day-to-day living. I will attempt to approach why this is from two angles – the religious and the cultural. I feel compelled to speak about death from these two perspectives because those of us from ethnic backgrounds will be able to relate to the experiences and observations I will share; my hope and heartfelt desire is that we will not be afraid to make the changes we so desperately need.

I am a Christian and have been practising for as long as I can remember. I think I have been quite fortunate that the main churches I have attended over the last 20+ years have been upstanding and not places of superstition and doom and gloom – the latter is not uncommon in some modern-day churches within parts of the black community. In Christianity, The Bible is a guide and sets the standard for Christian living. There are many scriptures and phrases that refer to promises of a long healthy life. As I have been a practising Christian for a while, I am very familiar with the teachings on this issue. It is also expected that as Christians, the belief is that one must live a life of faith for it to be a life that honours God and the teachings of Christ.

If we take Christianity for example, the Bible being the guide and standard set for Christian living, there are many scriptures and phrases that refer to promises of a long healthy life contained within; because I have been a practising Christian for a while, I am very familiar with the teachings of the Bible in this respect. It is also expected that as Christians, the belief is that one must live a life of faith for it to be a life that honours God and the teachings of Christ.

I'll give a little background to some fundamentals of the Christian faith to put into context why some people may struggle to plan for something that's not supposed to happen until they are old and grey. The ideal is that we make provision for when we die and ensure our loved ones are taken care of. This is particularly relevant to those of us in the diaspora with access to life insurance and written wills. If there are any disputes, the right channels can be accessed to resolve any issues arising through an incorruptible court system.

Chapter 19. A Penny for Your Thoughts

For a staunch Christian, the idea that one will 'die before their time' can be challenging to their beliefs, because it goes against the teachings of positive confessions and not walking in faith as this is displeasing to God; after all, The Bible does say, 'without faith it is impossible to please God.' It's easy to say this way of thinking is unrealistic or unreasonable but that is the very essence of what faith is. When you believe something strongly in your heart, you don't always need to see the evidence in front of you before you to have that belief confirmed. The problem here is in trying to bridge the gap between being a person of faith and being practical at the same time. Some of our religious practices have made us somewhat impractical in tackling day-to-day life issues such as sickness and death.

Whether we like it or not, some of us will fall sick and recover and some of us will fall sick and die. Some of us may die in seemingly good health – that is just the cold hard reality of life and no amount of faith can change that; it was just designed that way. Unfortunately, this isn't heaven – if you believe in heaven; here on Earth people lose their lives all the time. Good people, young people, children, husbands, wives, brothers, sisters, mothers and fathers; we just don't know when our time will come and therefore it's so important that we begin to have these conversations to put in place conscious plans on what we would like to happen in the event of our passing.

Because of our belief system, we are shy away from talking about death; many people believe if they speak about it seriously, they are tempting fate and will indeed die before their time. It would be helpful for spouses and partners, as well as the children that will be left behind, to be considered if the worst did happen. Of course, if you love someone you want to make sure they are protected, and one of the best ways may be to take out a life insurance policy. Other practical things like financial transparency between you and your spouse are important. There is only one thing worse than dealing with the loss of a loved one, and that's being left in debt or financial turmoil. I cannot imagine the stress, anguish and fear at a time of great loss and not being able to talk to the one person you would normally run to in tough situations. I believe financial worries really compound an already desperate situation and the solution to it doesn't have to be too complex or difficult.

The thoughts we might have about planning for death should gently be explored using the very teachings of The Bible through personal research. I am aware it speaks quite openly about death; in fact, The Bible speaks of leaving an inheritance for your children. That would intimate to me that the Bible is aware of the importance and necessity of provision after death. I believe inheritance is another word for provision and if you are married or have a partner you care about, then it would be the right thing to do to ensure their well-being after you have passed on, covering both your children and partner.

Culturally, within some of the West African communities I know of, the roles of the husbands and wives can be quite archaic. The position of the man as the head of the home can be misinterpreted and abused to insinuate that the man has complete autonomy over finances, especially if the wife doesn't work. The idea that the wife has a right to know about her husband's salary and other financial dealings is often a no-no. This is why a lot of women from such communities are left

Chapter 19. A Penny for Your Thoughts

financially vulnerable if the husband suddenly passes on after making no attempt to disclose to his wife where his money and assets are, in addition to not leaving a will.

There is a general mistrust within these marriages and some of it stems from what women are taught about marriage. Marriage is usually seen as the sole benefit to the woman as marriage validates and honours her, the same way that having children does. In such communities, these two things then become a standard by which a woman's worth is judged and if you cannot fulfil these expectations then you are not worthy. For this reason, many women will do whatever they can to stay married; no real responsibility goes to the husband to do his part to maintain a good marriage.

The issue this brings forth is a marriage where there is little or no trust, therefore discussing death, money, assets and inheritance is a complete no-go area. Why? The husband becomes suspicious of a wife who asks such questions because of course she must be plotting to kill him. In a society where husbands can never die of their own accord, what woman really wants to have these conversations? What if the husband mentions such a conversation to his family members and the unspeakable happens? The wife will be left in a very compromising position in having to explain how it was possible that she discussed assets with her husband and all of a sudden, he dies, even if sudden was 20 years later?

As much as I wish I had the power to change this very damaging mindset, I will appeal to those men who really do understand the meaning of marriage and genuinely love their wives and children to initiate a change. After my husband died, and after the treatment I was subjected to by certain family members, a thought came to my mind that I think could help cushion the blow for the family that is left behind. I had attempted to do this myself by suggesting a point of contact for the family, to save me having to be so present at a time of great anguish and turmoil. When marriages are conducted in Ghana, for example, even when a church wedding is performed, the customary or traditional marriage often takes place as well. I had a traditional wedding the week before Eddie and I officially got married. The traditional marriage is essentially done to introduce both families and for a dowry to be paid. Eddie did all of that very well and did me proud in terms of the things that were presented to my family to show that he was worthy of my hand in marriage. Whether the payment of a dowry is something one agrees with or not isn't really the focal point of what I am about to share. What it does is that it goes some way to indicate the intent of the man and his ability to fulfil the needs and requests of the family.

What I feel should be part of a marriage is identifying a person appointed to represent or care for the intended wife if the husband were to pass away. There are already family elders within each family in case there are issues in the marriage that may require family intervention (another topic for another day), but there isn't anyone specifically appointed for this purpose.

Why should this make a difference? Had this set-up existed in my case and for those of the women who shared their experiences with me, and elsewhere, it may have saved all of us from the abuse, vilification, victimisation, disrespect and distress. An appointed person would have shielded us from all that. Of course, this would not be without its complications.

Chapter 19. A Penny for Your Thoughts

All isn't lost though. I had a conversation about this very thing with a group of people and I put out my appeal to the men, not the women. I shared my experience that shocked them to their core. As I was seen as a strong woman, they couldn't imagine that I wasn't immune from a treatment that is the norm for women 'back home.' I asked them to imagine if it was their wife left to face this treatment amid trying not to lose their mind and look after their children. Worse still, if they didn't have children which usually affords a woman with a higher level of disrespect and viciousness. My question was "How would you want your wife to be treated?"

I was always Eddie's shield. Sometimes, it felt as if I was literally standing in front of him to protect him from an unknown enemy trying to take a shot, and I was ready to take the hit for him. This is how I feel a spouse should be protected from the elements of what is thrown their way by their in-laws. It may seem like something minor and of little value, but I can promise you, having someone from Eddie's family acting as an intermediary would have saved me a lot of stress and my children a lot of heartache.

When anyone challenges social issues or societal norms that are damaging, you automatically come across naysayers and those who want to maintain the *status quo* because that's how it has always been done. You cannot let that deter you. It takes just one person to say *no* because those who also want change will follow. It's not a numbers game. It's simply a game of making a change, of starting the change. Change one home, one family, one widow's life at a time with the hope there will eventually be a change in attitude that will be to the betterment of all.

I was humbled and more so relieved to have husbands contacting me saying they had never thought about half of the advice I'd given them. They had underestimated how important it was to make financial provision for their families if they died; furthermore, they had never thought about appointing a protector in the family to be a cushion if it was ever needed. Life insurance policies were being taken out and not just by husbands; single mothers were enquiring about taking out life insurance too, and wives were considering the urgency of writing their wills.

Of course, I don't have all the answers but if we don't talk it's unlikely we will find the solutions. This may be an opportunity for some of us to look at the condition and state of our marriages and start to repair any cracks. Life is short and unpredictable as we well know and if we use these opportunities to have the kinds of marriages that will allow transparency, then the time is now. No marriage is perfect, and Rome wasn't built in a day but if you have chosen to be with the person you're with, make it count and enjoy your life with them. Part of that enjoyment is securing and protecting their future as best as you can.

Chapter 20

New Beginnings

When you love someone and make the decision to spend the rest of your life with them, you never really make any allowances in your head, or your heart, that you won't grow old with them. If you say the conventional marriage vows, 'Till death do us part,' you don't really expect it to happen until you're both old and grey; it's just not something you think about. When they die prematurely and leave you all alone, what are you supposed to do with all your love and all those dreams you spoke about? It can be so daunting to even try to comprehend embarking on a relationship after losing your loved one and there are many reasons for this.

Before I go into those reasons, I would like to share what I feel is true of widows who may consider dating after being bereaved. Contrary to what people may think, I personally don't believe you forget the person you've lost because you have either remarried or started dating and we've seen the proof of that in Penelope's story.

After speaking to several widows who have remarried, it's evident that whatever emotions they held for their late husbands don't just evaporate. The love for a cherished husband who has gone too soon is immortalised. That love stands still in time. Those feelings don't disappear; they are ring-fenced and remain. It's a very difficult concept to explain, but this is the best I can do to convey what it's like.

I believe you grow another heart, one that has the capacity of loving and caring for a new person, but that very much runs parallel to the heart you gave your husband. I don't believe either heart has greater power over the other; there is no amount of grief that overshadows the new love in your life but neither can the new love in your life diminish the sense of loss or love for the one you have lost. Each heart lives with equal measures of joy and pain.

Having painted this picture, you are the only one who can determine when you are ready to embark on a new romance. It's not for anyone to impose an argument to the big question 'To date or not to date?' Indeed, that is the question, but it's the question only you should pose to yourself and only you should answer. I found it truly fascinating that people who would never, under normal circumstances, have a say in my love life, now brazenly offered advice, opinions and judgements for and against me dating, remarrying or remaining a widow. The sheer effrontery of it all! As a fully-grown woman, I was being told anything from "It's too soon to be thinking of dating now," to being coerced by many undesirables to opt for the type of relationships I would never have even considered as a young, single woman, let alone in my forties and widowed!

It's almost as if because you're widowed, you cease to be *corpus mentis*. It is so demeaning and disempowering to say the least and extremely patronising at best; if we were sensible

Chapter 20. New Beginnings

and able to make an independent decision to get married previously, why on earth are we suddenly incapable of making that decision for ourselves again?

This attitude and prejudice brings me onto something else – if I were a man, would these conversations be happening? It seems to be totally accepted within many societies for a man to be widowed and remarried, even if it's within a year of his wife's passing. Nobody bats an eyelid, and nobody questions if he's sure or ready. It's just taken for granted that a widower seems to have more needs than a widow. Therefore, society is much kinder to him than a woman who has lost her husband.

I know for a fact that if a woman from my community, for example, was widowed, and had the audacity to marry within a year of her husband's passing, there would be accusations ranging from her carrying on behind her husband's back to her being a witch and killing him. Of course, in Africa men never just die as I mentioned earlier; their wives must have killed them with witchcraft. Gender inequality is really a thing, even when it comes to death.

Imagine facing something as devastating as losing your husband and yet there are those who would rather you wallow in loneliness and misery than find love again and be happy. Of course, I make this statement for those who wish to love again, and not those who by choice wish to remain as they are. The key point to this is choice; it's our choice how we wish to live.

I have also been struck by how few people consider what it feels like for a woman to have been married, with all the perks that marriage brings, to now having to readjust to a new version of themselves they didn't ask for. Let me speak generally here. When you're in a good marriage, you have compassion on tap, company on tap, a shoulder to cry on tap, and sex on tap! Yes, I said it, *sex*. We don't ever consider what it feels like for a woman who was used to enjoying the sexual side of her marriage to suddenly having to forego it for good. The idea of course is that good and decent women shouldn't enjoy sex or put any emphasis on that part of our needs. Once your husband dies, so should your sex drive, and any essence of you that is sexual or loving; it's a myth as well as a fallacy. We cannot speak about those needs because the idealistic part of the romanticised version of widowhood is written such that you shouldn't desire any man other than your husband. Though this may very well be true for some, and I have spoken to a few, it isn't the same for everyone. However, the feelings of condemnation and judgement of self and from others, stops many women from embarking or entertaining a relationship, no matter how long it is after being bereaved.

There is nothing lonelier than lying alone in a bed you've shared with your husband for years and look at the empty pillow where his head used to lay. God showed me a little mercy in my case because, for the previous nearly four years, Eddie was in the converted living room. When he died, I was grateful that we had that 'separation' because I really don't know what I would have done otherwise.

We face many barriers to happiness after bereavement, and we need to challenge the traditional, cultural and societal pressures imposed against that happiness. Few women have the strength to say no or to go against the grain because they still rely heavily on family support. How painful for the love and commitment to your husband's memory to be tainted with false stories of infidelity, such as in Afi's experience.

Chapter 20. New Beginnings

Hearing her sobs as she recounted the denial of the child she was carrying for her husband has affected her many years later; my own heart broke for her, imagining what it would have been like to go through that experience.

We really don't morph into being different people in the typical sense, because we have lost a husband. We are still here. It is so frustrating to suddenly lose yourself and not be seen. Your whole identity is wrapped up in just being the widow. Nobody looks at you the same way anymore, and you're lucky if people even remember your name. You're the woman that lost her husband; your name immediately become irrelevant. We don't realise how symbolic this is, but I think I have come to understand where the problem may arise. The stereotypes that surround that status are what make people think in a certain way and try to make you fit into their definition of widowhood; the painted picture is of a woman in a constant state of mourning – reflected in how we dress, how often we laugh and how long we remain single for.

A woman who has loved and lost in this way and is able to love again is a pretty good catch if you ask me. Why? I believe it takes a lot to get to the point to even attempt to try. It's frightening and it's fraught with 101 reasons why you shouldn't do it – from wondering if you can love that deeply again to worrying about what would happen if you lost another person you loved. It's not an easy place to be, especially if you begin to harbour feelings of guilt for even thinking about it. Many women speak of feeling as if they are being unfaithful to their husband by wanting to date again.

I think the person who wants to date a woman who has been widowed needs to tread gently; being single is a strange place to be for a widow and the last thing that's needed is pressure. For you the widow, be kind and gentle to yourself once you decide to date again, or if the prospect of dating comes your way. You shouldn't feel rushed or pressurised – if it does then maybe you aren't ready; it must feel right.

There are some opportunists out there waiting for a woman they feel is vulnerable and can take advantage of. That's a real fear for a widow. Nobody wants to fall into the wrong hands the first time you start dating. It's an already humungous step to take and shouldn't be taken lightly for the person who is bereaved and the person who wants to have a relationship with her. Any relationship isn't really going to be between the two parties…to a degree. The person who died wasn't just a husband; they were a friend, an in-law and possibly a father too. There are all these other people who will want to see who this new person is and if they fit into their lives, as well as your life. By no means is this an easy situation to walk into but if the intentions are honourable and both parties are clear on what they want, it can really work. It can help to put yourself in the other person's shoes too. There should be no comparisons because that wouldn't be fair, not to you or the person you're with. You can't replace the person you've lost and the person you're with shouldn't feel that they must do that either.

Something that I feel is important is being open and honest about your feelings regarding the loss. We tend to not want to make the person feel second best or walk in the shadow of the husband who has died. In all honesty, you should be able to speak about your late husband guilt-free and without pretending you won't have sad times. Wedding anniversaries, birthdays and Father's Day are days where you might not

Chapter 20. New Beginnings

feel your best and you should be able to be expressive during those times. Suppressing how you feel also means you're not being authentic and true to yourself, and that's not a good recipe for a healthy relationship. If you feel you must hide your feelings for any reason, you may need to be honest with yourself and decide if you really are with the right person. Whatever the challenges and outcome, starting to date again is a positive move; you at the very least prove you have the emotional capacity to date again, and that is huge.

There is life after being a widow. It is extremely difficult, and I don't have the luxury of saying any different. It's a road full of twists and turns and untold uncertainty. I have never thought about death so often as I have after I lost my husband. I do think if he could leave so suddenly, who am I to not come up against the same fate? There is all that to deal with and sometimes, in the rubble of grief and trying to climb out of it, we don't afford ourselves enough time to see the light that's trying to come through the debris. Life, by its very nature, is full of uncertainty and we cannot possibly plan for every eventuality, so what are we going to do?

We may not know the reason but there is a reason why we are still here, and we must make our existence count. We do ourselves, our loved ones and especially our husbands who have embarked on their next journey, a great disservice by curling up and dying. We are still here. Let's make the rest of our lives count, in whatever way we can, to bring us some joy before our time comes.

What happened to me is the worst thing that I could ever have imagined. I had to grab the worst that life had to throw at me. No warning, no notice and certainly no permission from me. If this same life throws me love with no warning, no notice and no permission, I'll grab it with the same dignity and grace I dealt with death, recognising that essentially this is how life goes. The only control you have is how you respond to what life brings your way; your only choice is how you deal with it. Life is way too short and if you're blessed enough to love again, if you're blessed enough to live again, stretch out your hands and grab it, guilt and shame-free.

★★★

Eddie, I was blessed enough to experience everything I vowed to you in July of 2005. 'Till death us do part' happened sooner than I ever thought possible, but your love has propelled me into this place of grace. I am still here, and I promise to live for the both of us and bask in all that life has to offer. Continue to rest in perfect peace.

Acknowledgements

It is only by grace that I was able to write this book. I thank the Lord for the strength to do so. The many times I asked why I was suffering this fate, I have reluctantly accepted that you needed my voice beyond my words and human understanding. You needed my heart, so here I am Lord. In all things I give thanks.

I would like to take this opportunity to give heartfelt and sincere thanks to the following people that made this very painful journey easier than it would have been without their contributions, love, support, patience and encouragement:

A huge thanks to my Mum, Agnes Duku, who despite being so worried about her last daughter, has always had a word of encouragement for me whilst writing this book and constantly tells me how proud she is of me. At a time where I doubted my very existence, her love and support has been priceless.

My father Nicholas Duku, aka my twin – whose quiet, gentle support did not go unnoticed and was much appreciated.

My children Omar and Isobel, for putting up with my moods in dealing with the many times I had to withdraw to gather my thoughts. They are the two most amazing children any mother could wish for and I'm grateful that Eddie left a part of himself in them. I love you two, but you still drive me nuts, yet I wouldn't change you for the world.

My sister Jacqueline Pianim, for taking time to read excerpts of the book to help me articulate my thoughts.

To the four amazing women who selflessly shared their stories on their grief journey with me for the benefit of others. You bared your souls to show that one widow, that one child, is not invisible; their voice matters. I pray your own journeys continue in grace and strength always.

Special thanks to Shelly Herman whose counselling support made writing this book so much more bearable. I am grateful for the Thursday mornings that allowed me to be my authentic self no matter what I wanted to share. The times where reliving this ordeal would make me physically ill would be eased by the perspective you helped me gain. You may have been doing your job but for me it has given me a part of my life back – thank you.

I couldn't possibly forget the Conscious Dreams Publishing team. Thank you from the bottom of my heart for the respect and sensitivity you have shown me throughout this journey. Special thanks to Daniella Blechner for giving me such support when it all got too much for me. I won't forget how you told me to take my time and not put myself through the ringer to get this book done if it was making me so ill. I'm grateful for your friendship and belief in me that I could do this.

A book needs a good editor to bring everything together and still have your voice shine through. I thank Lee Dickinson and Rhoda Molife for their meticulous work in ensuring that's exactly what happened. Thank you, Oksana Kosovan, for your great typesetting work which I appreciate very much.

Heartfelt thanks to Lawrence Coke for your creativity, sensitivity, respect and kindness when coming up with the concept for the trailer of this book. It's the little things that often aren't that little and have the greatest impact.

I cannot thank Joe Mensah enough for not only being a great photographer but also for being the photographer who captured the picture of me reading my tribute to my husband that has now become the cover of this book. It is a picture that speaks a thousand words. The shot also speaks not only of your talent but also of how well you understood my emotions and how you immortalised them. You've been my photographer for many years now and as the years go on, I am more amazed at how you can capture such deep moments and yet make your presence almost invisible; I am thankful to you for your support.

To my special girls:

I would like to thank my darling Patricia Daniels who has been more than a sister to me, taking my daily calls without fail and letting me bend her ear about how painful this process has been. Thank you for spurring me on.

Thank you to Sharlene Appiah whose moral support has been invaluable; I appreciate you endlessly. Friendship really isn't defined by time.

Marilyn Danso and I have been friends for a long time, and I know even speaking about this book has been a challenge for her. Thank you for being there for me always. Thank you for times past, present and in the future.

Anita Aggrey, thank you. Under different circumstances you would have helped edit such an important book, but it was way too close to home for you. I appreciate all that you are to me.

Simone Brown, I have grown to love you so much over the last year. Thank you for just being there and helping with transcribing some of the stories of these brave women. You've made me laugh with your cheekiness and so much more that I can't write here.

And finally, to my dear aunt-in-law, Mrs Mameh Saracoulli – Aunty in this book – who sadly passed away on Saturday 21 December 2019. You were Eddie's favourite and mine too. You welcomed me into the family with open arms and a pure heart. Your love and support was always appreciated. I will truly and sincerely miss you. God bless you Aunty Mameh.

About the Author

Dilys Sillah is a Transformational Life Coach specialising in emotional independence and relationship coaching. She is a TEDx speaker and founder of former charity Who Will Hear My Cry (WWHMC) that raised awareness on rape, child abuse and domestic violence.

Not This Widow – A Journey Of Grief: Love, Loss, Strength and Survival is her second book. Her first is *Predator or Prince: How To Find The Man Of Your Dreams, Not Your Nightmares* which educates women on how to spot red flags in men who may be emotionally or physically abusive.

Dilys began her writing journey as an advocate for abused women and children. Her profession as a coach gave her insight into the challenges that come with recovering from trauma, failed and unhealthy relationships and how people bounce back from those experiences or not.

Her passion to support women to build self-confidence, self-esteem and stand against societal or cultural stereotypes laid the foundation for her greatest test. She was unexpectedly widowed and introduced to the world of victimisation, isolation and profound grief. All these factors inspired her to fight another cause for not only widows but also for those who have lost a loved one and want to grieve authentically, but don't know how.

Dilys lives and works from her home in London and enjoys travelling, meeting new people and singing – the latter she did professionally. She has shared the stage with some gospel and R&B greats and was a backing vocalist on a number one single in the 90s ironically called 'Things Can Only Get Better' by D:Ream.

Conscious Dreams
PUBLISHING

Transforming diverse writers
into successful published authors

www.consciousdreamspublishing.com

authors@consciousdreamspublishing.com

Let's connect

www.ingramcontent.com/pod-product-compliance
Lightning Source LLC
Chambersburg PA
CBHW030036100526
44590CB00011B/221